agile business for
FRAGILE TIMES

....

*Strategies for Enhancing
Competitive Resiliency and
Stakeholder Trust*

Mary Pat McCarthy
Jeff Stein

with Rob Brownstein

....

McGraw-Hill

New York   Chicago   San Francisco   Lisbon
London   Madrid   Mexico City   Milan
New Delhi   San Juan   Seoul
Singapore   Sydney   Toronto

*The **McGraw·Hill** Companies*

1 2 3 4 5 6 7 8 9 0 AGM/AGM 0 9 8 7 6 5 4 3 2 1

ISBN 0-07-140084-2

Production services provided by CWL Publishing Enterprises, Madison, WI, www.cwlpub.com.

All information provided is of a general nature and is not intended to address the circumstances of any particular individual or entity. Although we endeavor to provide accurate and timely information, there can be no guarantee that such information is accurate as of the date it is received or that it will continue to be accurate in the future. No one should act upon such information without appropriate professional advice after a thorough examination of the facts of a particular situation.

McGraw-Hill books are available at special quantity discounts to use as premiums and sales promotions, or for use in corporate training sessions. For more information, please write to the Director of Special Sales, Professional Publishing, McGraw-Hill, Two Penn Plaza, New York, NY 10121-2298. Or contact your local bookstore.

 This book is printed on recycled, acid-free paper containing a minimum of 50% recycled de-inked fiber.

Contents

Foreword

History is easy to study but hard to live by. In every era of technological change, every era of new and exciting possibilities, the lessons of history are glanced at and then disregarded. That was then, it is said, and this is now, and now is different. We are in a new economy, the gurus cried ... in the 1920s, the 1960s, and the late 1990s, one in which new rules apply, one in which business is changing faster than ever before, one in which either you get it or you don't. And there is always a grain of truth to the claim. But only a grain.

During periods of technological and financial euphoria, the pressure to conform is immense. So is the temptation: the stockmarkets reward those who appear to play by the new rules. By making capital apparently free to those in the vanguard, the markets amplify the trend. They also induce plenty of people and organizations to bend or even break the rules in order to exploit the excitement, or to seem to be part of it. But then something else has always happened, in every financial boom of the 20th century: reality has reasserted itself, and the markets have crashed. Suddenly, the new economy has turned old. And at such moments the claim that business is changing faster than ever before becomes abruptly and dangerously true. Those able to adapt to the change survive. Many, however, do not.

The reason why these booms and busts happen was put most succinctly by Arthur C. Clarke, author of *2001: A Space Odyssey* and conceiver of satellite communications. Typically, he observed, we *over*estimate the speed and impact of technological change in the short term but *under*estimate it in the long term. The electric telegraph, railways, electrification, radio and most recently the Internet have all caused huge excitement about imminent change, followed by financial collapses and disappointment. Eventually, though, the predictions came true. These technologies did transform the world. It was just that human affairs took longer to adjust to or exploit the discoveries of science than the enthusiasts expected.

Such times have always posed tough problems for businesses. The conventional time horizons become inverted. Companies need to position themselves for the long term, but meanwhile keep making money every month and every day. But as technological excitement takes hold, the long-term strategic tasks seem to become telescoped into short-term ones, interfering with the normal, tactical operations of businesses. During the 1990s, that difficulty of balancing the short and long terms became complicated even further by intensifying competition in increasingly open and global markets.

The greatest paradox, perhaps, of technologically driven booms and busts is that times that are nominally being shaped by deep thought and new ideas actually become characterized by too little thought and by too much conformity. The old slogan at IBM, "Think," is easily ignored.

The purpose of *The Economist* is to keep that slogan alive, to help our readers to think issues through, even if those readers do not necessarily agree with our conclusions. The same is true of this book. As booms go and busts come, managers need to be agile. Lessons can be learned from history, and from the case studies in this book. You do not have to agree with all the conclusions. But it will help you to think.

Bill Emmott, Editor
The Economist

Introduction

During a robust economic expansion, it's hard to make a serious blunder. A mistake here or there is typically hidden by abundant growth. But when the economy contracts, and revenues turn south, the true measure of a company's resiliency is revealed.

Which "agile" companies seem to ride out the storm in better shape than others? What are they doing to more effectively manage during fragile times? What strategies are they employing in planning for a return to growth? Which of their agile strategies are applicable and effective regardless of changing economic conditions?

The downturn of 2001 was an opportune time to explore these and other questions. Revenues declined in all sectors everywhere in the world. This gave us a chance to examine companies of every stripe and to look at their performances both domestically and globally. This book is the output of that examination and consideration.

In the first chapter, we look at

- ❑ The manifestation of agility
- ❑ The common denominators that characterize agile businesses

❏ The factors over which management can exert some influence or control

Differences in philosophy affect how companies address their problems. Some see a glass that is emptying; others see one ready to be filled. And those views heavily influence their responses to the problem of balancing revenues and costs. Where some companies see problems, others see opportunities. Where some companies focus only six months out, others pay homage to longer-term objectives while still dealing with short-term priorities. Where some companies apply across-the-board budget cuts, others take a more deliberative approach and even increase investments in some instances. While companies in a global economy as diverse as ours clearly display qualities and needs that are unique to their market, their industry, or their culture, we were interested to note that those businesses that seem to have fared the best all share certain key characteristics. Examining those characteristics, we realized they were applicable to many companies in most industries.

First of these is the strength of the company's management, specifically the chief executive. Chapter two examines the agility requirements that chief executives will increasingly be called on to tackle. These include:

❏ The changing measures of success
❏ Making shareholder value more than a cliché
❏ Authenticity, trust, and good corporate citizenship
❏ Fostering an environment that promotes business agility

No industry is immune from innovation and change, but

some companies are habitually more successful in responding to fluctuating and evolving market conditions. They do this by continually challenging conventional wisdom. Chapter three provides an opportunity for reflection on this point:

❑ What have we learned from the recent boom and bust?
❑ Which bits of conventional wisdom remain steadfastly valid?
❑ Which have been debunked?

The term "cycle" implies repetition, and economies continue to cycle through expansions and contractions. But each cycle has its own unique aspects, and the pace of innovation plays a part in their respective length and magnitude. As a result, each up or down curve brings with it the cumulative wisdom of the past. It is up to agile businesses to distill from that experience those innovations and strategies that offer the best route to competitive sustainability.

Chapter four is about the role of information sharing and communication in enabling business agility. It addresses the role of internal and external communications in:

❑ Defining market perception and opportunity
❑ Establishing a canvas that promotes credibility
❑ Reinforcing brand and relevancy

Agile businesses all seem to share a thirst for leveraging communications from a mundane function into an active source of strategic advantage. They do so with strong participation and commitment at the highest levels of the organization.

Chapter five looks at strategy against a backdrop of increasing uncertainty. Rather than defining carefully planned, "one-strike" immutable solutions, agile businesses focus management attention on sculpting a series of defensible alternatives. This chapter examines three broad strategic stances that companies can take:

❏ Transformer
❏ Adapter
❏ Equivocal-intent-to-participate

All three are examined in terms of levels of risk/reward and their prudent application under varying degrees of uncertainty.

Chapter six goes the next step. A great strategy is only as good as its execution. Agile businesses are distinguished by their performance cultures. In this chapter we look at what it takes to build one successfully:

❏ Prudent strategy and clear description
❏ A performance team
❏ Appropriate measurement and reward systems

Chapter seven looks at contrarian behavior during fragile times, in particular at companies that:

❏ Spend against the tide
❏ Innovate instead of hibernate
❏ Expand when others are cutting back

It takes courage to act in a way that is boldly contrary to prevailing business custom, but such contrarian strategies, when executed well, are supported by solid principles and a growing history of positive results.

Chapter eight examines ways of balancing revenues and costs while minimizing the risks of later competitive disadvantage. It looks at:

❑ Creative ways of reducing costs without hobbling operations
❑ Thoughtful ways of better leveraging existing resources
❑ The importance of cash and ways of creating a cash cushion

In chapter nine we look to several CEOs who doggedly plan for growth regardless of the economic climate. Their experience and success grounded on:

❑ Continual innovation
❑ Constant streamlining and efficiency pursuits
❑ Establishing a flexible cost structure
❑ Revenue growth plans congruent with cost-reduction plans

This chapter reveals more ways to preserve competitiveness while dealing with the short-term interruptions in revenue streams.

Chapter ten, in the spirit of creativity, innovation, and alternative strategies, looks at how some companies are changing their value models to reflect the changes in customer wants and needs. It focuses on:

❑ Changing business models
❑ The rise of the intangible
❑ Making value more transparent

Given changing economics and customer needs, some companies choose to wait out the storm and hope for things to revert to pre-storm value models and propositions. Other companies take advantage of the tumult to revise and improve the value proposition. The idea is if something can be made a better value during hard times, it will have even greater value when conditions improve.

Chapter eleven presents some final conclusions and industry insights. The objective for this last chapter, as it is with the book as a whole, is to offer alternatives to the usual prescriptions for proceeding through economic volatility. This commentary is considerably enriched by the gracious contribution of so many CEOs who generously agreed to share their insights and experience. We hope you enjoy.

Acknowledgments

This book could not have been written without the candid and insightful interviews provided by Ed Breen, former President and COO of Motorola; Jeffrey Eisenach, President of the Progress & Freedom Foundation; Sir Christopher Gent, CEO of Vodafone; Thomas Glocer, CEO of Reuters; Baruch Lev, Bardes Professor of Accounting at New York University's Stern School of Business; Terry McGraw, CEO of McGraw-Hill; Garry McGuire, CFO of Avaya; James Morgan, CEO of Applied Materials; Thomas Ryder, CEO of Reader's Digest; and Carl Vogel, CEO of Charter Communications.

We are indebted to these executives whose stories and experience informed and greatly enriched our publication. Our partners Barbara Carbone, Mark Carleton, Dale Currie, Tim Flynn, Thomas Garigliano, Carl Geppert, Alistair Johnston, Shaun Kelly, Dale LeMasters, Gary Matuszak, Joe Mauriello, Jack Miller, Tom Moser, Gene O'Kelly, Tim Pearson, Terri Santisi, Richard Smith and Ashley Steel were a generous source of information and support and gave valuable assistance at critical stages of the book's development. We are also grateful to Sandra Kresch for providing a sounding board of ideas and suggestions, and to Jil Polniak for her capable and thoughtful review. Rob Brownstein and Marie Glenn contributed much to the writing of this document. Thank you all.

Mary Pat McCarthy

Jeff Stein

June 2002

Also co-authored by Mary Pat McCarthy

Digital Transformation: The Essentials of e-Business Leadership

Security Transformation: Digital Defense Strategies to Protect Your Company's Reputation and Market Share

CHAPTER ONE

Not Business as Usual

March 7, 2000—An ominous turn

Richard Conroy's Bose Wave® radio/CD player turned on at precisely 5:45 a.m., waking him to sounds of the Rippingtons. The CEO of Corinthian Systems rolled out of bed and headed straight for the master bathroom for his morning shower and shave. As he was finishing shaving, he reached across with his left arm to stretch the skin over his right cheekbone and mowed down the stubble with his Bosch electric razor. "Another day, another two million dollars," he said with a sigh as he made sure his face was now shaved clean.

Corinthian Systems had just passed an annual sales run rate of $730 million and all indicators continued to point upward. Tuesdays tended to be less hectic than Mondays and this one appeared to be no exception. At yesterday's senior management meeting, Conroy reiterated to his vice presidents of Marketing, Sales, Finance, Engineering, and Manufacturing that the boom would not go on forever.

"We're going to have an industry downturn," he said with conviction. "It's just a question of when and how deep,"

Conroy added emphatically. Then, they proceeded to review the latest financial performance data and compare the results with their quarter's short-term objectives. Revenues were higher than planned, but so were costs. "I don't want you to take your eyes off our cost-management goals," chided Conroy. "At some point investors will start looking at the bottom lines, again." The meeting concluded.

Today, Conroy was scheduled for an 11 a.m. interview with an editor from *Fortune* magazine; a 12:30 to 2:30 p.m. lunch with Bill Dabney, the CEO of Warner Electronics, one of Corinthian's largest suppliers; a 3:30 p.m. meeting with Cole Vincent, CEO of TeleMart Corp., one of Corinthian's largest customers; and, if no alarm claxons began sounding, Conroy just might have a chance to see that basketball game at Stanford starting at 7 p.m.

At the interview with *Fortune*, the editor asked about the dot.com market. "This is a market with nearly $700 billion in capitalization and about $6 billion in revenues, most of it from Yahoo! and AOL. It's ripe for a major correction, don't you think?" he asked Conroy.

"It scares me," the CEO replied. "It has all the classic earmarks of a speculative bubble and I think a lot of investors—including institutional investors—are going to get hurt when it pops."

"So, what does Corinthian do to avoid getting hurt if revenues suddenly plummet?" the editor continued.

"We take a very conservative approach to projecting business and estimating revenues," Conroy answered. "In that way, we hope to avoid excess spending in advance of questionable revenues. We also make sure that order and payment risks are appropriately managed." He made a mental note to remind Chuck Wills, his chief operating officer, that no matter how hard Sales might push to relax credit standards for start-up customers, he wanted the company to stand fast. The interview wrapped up a short time later and Conroy headed on to his lunch appointment.

At lunch, Conroy found out that the five-week supplier backlog could now be sliced in half. "Actually, I can deliver in less than three weeks, now," Dabney told him. "The backlog critical path has been components from two of our vendors. Two days ago, both told me they can now supply in one week instead of three. Rumor has it that Argo Technologies had ordered a huge quantity of these parts and then cancelled suddenly."

Just as Dabney finished, Conroy felt his beeper vibrate in his shirt pocket. He said, "Excuse me for a second, Bill," and looked at the number. Conroy pulled the cell phone out of his jacket pocket and pressed Mark Croyden's speed-dial number in the "war room" at Corinthian.

"Mark," said Conroy.

"The Dow sank nearly 375 points at close, today," said Croyden.

"Call a War Room meeting for 5:30 p.m., Mark," Conroy ordered after a second's hesitation. Well, there goes the basketball game, thought Conroy, as he put the cell phone away.

"Anything exciting?" asked Dabney.

"It just might be," Conroy nodded.

March 7, 2000: The War Room at Corinthian—Fast response

"Two things happened today that may affect our business in a big way," Conroy began. He looked from face to face at the six people sitting around the table now looking at him. "The Dow sank big time, today. And one of our suppliers is reporting much shorter backlogs.

"Now," Conroy continued, "the Dow thing may just be short-term jitters. But a lot of these start-up companies have been ordering on the basis of capitalization, not revenues. Tomorrow, I want us to go through all recent deliveries and pending orders and recalculate payment and order-cancellation risks. I want to see worst-case analysis of what it does to quarterly revenues and earnings. Then, I want all of you to go through your current budgets and plans and reconsider priorities and totals. On Thursday morning, clear your calendars and we'll meet, here, at 7:30 a.m. Any questions?"

"Richard, I've been keeping my eyes on the daily sales reports and I'm not seeing any evidence of softening, yet," Ken Kamper, VP of Sales, interjected.

"That's great, Ken," Conroy replied, "and keep doing exactly that. I want to know as soon as anyone sees something odd."

"Richard, Warner isn't the only vendor that's starting to shorten up the backlog," said Ravi Kalkar, VP of Manufacturing. "Two other vendors are showing sudden capacity too. I'll dig a little and see if I can find out what's behind it."

"That's super, Ravi. And, Ken, don't wait for the dailies. Call some of your regional guys and ask them if they sense anything changing," said Conroy.

"Anything else?" Conroy looked around from face to face, again.

"OK. That's it. We'll meet again, here, Thursday morning," Conroy stood up. "Thanks, guys."

March 16, 2000—Continued vigilance

A week had passed since the follow-up War Room meeting that Thursday morning. Conroy had gotten what he asked for and all of his senior managers now shared their CEO's heightened sensitivity to rumblings in the supply chain and customer base. Mark Croyden was Conroy's "intelligence officer." He was responsible for building Corinthian's finely tuned business information system. An ardent believer in the power and advantage of digital transformation, Conroy had commissioned Croyden to help define and then oversee the company's online universe.

It linked Corinthian with its suppliers and customers, permitting both to see, in near real time, the information critical to making informed decisions. Suppliers were also networked with Corinthian's engineering division so that proposed engineering changes could be quickly evaluated in terms of cost and implementation time. In addition, Corinthian's customer relationship management (CRM) system was linked with online and call-center customer support, so that potential problems were detected quickly and resolved before they could grow.

Croyden was also responsible for other intelligence. His team kept an ongoing vigil on macroeconomic trends, such as currency fluctuation, legislative activity, the jobs report, productivity and costs, producer and consumer price indices, and other indicators. It was the team's job to sift through the volumes of information it received and alert Conroy and his executive team about any disturbing findings.

Today's meeting was set for 2:30 p.m. and, as he walked to his chair, the CEO exclaimed, "The Dow closed up over 499 points, today. So, should we just adjourn this meeting?" he asked with a smile.

"It's like I told you on Tuesday, Richard,"answered the CFO, Neil DiSimone. "There's no other place for the institutional investors to go. We don't have to worry about a prolonged market crash. Things will be volatile for a while, but the bull's not dead, yet."

"Maybe the bull's not dead," Kalkar (VP, Manufacturing) weighed in, "but practically every one of our suppliers is talking about sudden increases in supply and practically same-day delivery. I know it's not because their vendors have all become incredibly productive. Lots of big customers are cutting back on lots of big orders and component supplier inventories are suddenly growing."

"I'm still not seeing big changes in the sales dailies," added Kamper (VP, Sales), "but some of our mid-size prospects are now pushing back on placing orders this quarter."

"OK," said Conroy. "My gut is telling me there's going to be some rough quarters ahead of us. Greenspan has been ratcheting up the interest rates, oil prices have tripled in recent months, and we're seeing yield inversion in bonds. If you do your history homework, you'll see that in combination these factors have preceded six of the last eight recessions. So, while I'm not saying we're going to have a recession, I am saying that the odds are increasing. If we're on the cusp of a downturn—and I think we are—we've got to make sure we're prepared with shifts in strategy that put us at less risk."

April 14, 2000—Another shoe drops; responsiveness continues
In the ensuing weeks, stock market volatility continued. There was now a clearly discernible softening in supplier backlogs and customer orders. Some new product introductions were being delayed and some R&D projects were being scrapped. Key technical personnel on scrapped projects were being reassigned to others. Filling open jobs in specific areas of the company was now suspended.

On April 14, 2000, the Dow Jones Industrial Average plunged 617.78 points, a loss of 6.7%. Whereas the Dow would return to 10,000 and above, the NASDAQ would have a mostly downward slide, giving back over $2 trillion in share-price appreciation.

Before March, Corinthian's management had set goals that were about equally balanced between top-line growth and bottom-line earnings. They had revised that plan to focus more on earnings and less on growth. In addition, Conroy and his executives were looking for ways of turning a greater percentage of revenues into cash and were trying to increase the proportion of sales through their channel partners as a way to speed up the sales cycle, lower the cost of sales, and increase revenues even during a downturn.

April 15, 2000 and beyond—Contrarian behavior

While other CEOs became less accessible to employees, shareholders, analysts, and editors, Richard Conroy increased his exposure to all these audiences. He wrote frequent e-mails to his employees, giving them the latest assessment of company progress, and made sure his executives and managers remained proactive in detecting and responding to employee fears. Conroy continued to make himself available for press interviews and charged his marketing communications department with finding suitable speaking opportunities.

Corinthian Systems increased its advertising budget over that of 1999, using a greater proportion of funds for product and corporate brand management. As before, new strategic initiatives were structured such that they could be effectively steered, midcourse, as related factors changed unpredictably.

Corinthian, like its competitors, saw its revenues decrease in 2001, but its earnings were consistent with 1999 and 2000 because the company practiced continuous cost management. Some of the more ambitious R&D projects were scrapped or postponed, but Corinthian remained committed to those considered high priority and core to the business before the downturn. As a result, the company was well positioned to compete effectively once demand began to heat up again.

AGILE BUSINESSES

You won't find Corinthian Systems in any stock symbol look-up table and Richard Conroy won't be featured on the cover of *Forbes*. They are a compilation of CEOs and companies we researched in writing this book. These companies represent a range of sizes, years in business, vision, industry sectors, and financial strength. But, they are notable for their common ability to maintain a steady course in the face of economic change—positive, as in our recent bull market, or negative, as in the slump that has succeeded it.

> **Agile businesses are notable for their common ability to maintain a steady course in the face of economic change.**

We call this ability *business agility*. By most measures, qualitative and quantitative, agile businesses of comparable size and sector outperform less nimble competitors by:

❏ Maintaining a continual focus on profitability and revenue growth;

❏ Understanding central priorities and the importance of assessing and reporting on value;

❏ A sustaining commitment to communications that started at the top;

❏ Acquiring and filtering pertinent information from and to key constituents, rapidly;

❏ Testing assumptions and frequently measuring results;

❏ Having a performance culture;

❏ Enabling shared decision making; and

❏ Adapting rapidly to change.

These qualities give agile businesses a survivability edge that allows them to observe, react, and factor market changes into an embedded discipline of continual cost and growth refinement. In this way, leading companies set the stage for consistent, measured growth and sustainable profitability.

As you read further, you will find that business agility is not a one-man show. It is the combined effort of teams of people serving in every business discipline. Like most things pervasive, business agility starts at the top. Without total CEO commitment, it usually ends up half-baked. Consequently, we will examine several aspects of business agility in this book, viewed largely from a CEO perspective.

AGILE DISCIPLINES

Many of the agile executives we spoke with agree firmly that you build a company for the long term, despite short-term economic upheaval. That's a disciplined perspective, and we singularly agree. Our research and interviews support the view that businesses that strive for consistent, steady growth are those most likely to weather economic volatility with the least internal and external damage. It is the most prudent strategy.

The concept of enabling business agility is more than just a nice concept for nice times. The ability to adapt quickly in seizing and leveraging opportunity is a critical enabler to strategic and operational success. Truly agile businesses share a number of important qualities and behaviors. Among them are:

- ❑ Critical thinking and asking the right questions,
- ❑ Focusing on value and profitability,
- ❑ Adapting quickly to change,
- ❑ Building flexible, integrated processes,
- ❑ Being lean and disciplined,
- ❑ Acting reflectively, rather than reflexively,
- ❑ Instilling trust in constituents,
- ❑ Passionately creating alternatives, and
- ❑ Diligently measuring results and learning from them.

These concepts form the underpinning of an agile enterprise—and they also form the context for some of the discussion in this book—but clearly no company exhibits all to the same degree. The goal instead will be to map one's current organizational aptitudes and objectives to determine which of these areas are most meaningful and which are most in need of attention.

FRICTION: THE IMPEDIMENTS

Business agility implies an ability to move unshackled from impediments and constraints that would ordinarily weigh down an enterprise. We call such impediments *friction*.

> **Business agility implies an ability to move unshackled from impediments and constraints that would ordinarily weigh down an enterprise.**

There are a great number of areas of business friction and, like every facet of business, these evolve. Nonetheless, we have found that many boil down to the following core set. Some impediments are subject to control by companies and their CEOs; others are not.

Impediments that *can* be controlled:

- ❑ Corporate psychology (e.g., fear of failure),
- ❑ Perception of limited options,
- ❑ Corporate culture (e.g., inward-facing or rooted to the past),
- ❑ Poorly understood and valued assets,
- ❑ Suboptimal digital transformation, and
- ❑ Poorly understood risks.

Impediments that *cannot* be controlled:

- ❑ Economic turbulence,
- ❑ Market skepticism,
- ❑ Share-price volatility, and
- ❑ Government regulation.

These issues collectively and individually act as a brake on a company's otherwise free movement. They are curbs on momentum. There is effectively little one can do about impediments in the second list. But companies can control those on the first. Not doing so leads to competitive disadvantage.

For example, if a company's managers perceive limited options, then moves are limited, too. A corporate culture that dwells on the past or is not customer facing will be at a competitive disadvantage to those that are more customer-oriented and those that embrace change. Moreover, many CEOs prefer to keep intangible investments off the balance sheet and out of mind. But that can work against the cost of financing by giving prospective creditors a distorted sense of value.

Also, many companies have begun their digital transformations, but most still suffer from a lot of unfilled potential. For companies that press ahead and connect all the dots, digital transformation's positive impact on business agility can be there for the taking, too.

A PATH OF LESSER RESISTANCE

By understanding friction factors, companies can find ways of reducing their effects. In essence, they create for themselves paths of less resistance. Whereas taking a path of less resistance is often lumped with making compromises, in these cases it is aimed at increasing the odds of success by limiting energy-sapping obstacles.

For example, in the late 1970s, the personal computer market was still embryonic. But IBM saw the opportunity in it. The company also saw a number of problem areas that could impede its entry into that developing market. It took a step uncharacteristic for IBM then. It created an arm's-length skunk works project and located it 1200 miles away from Armonk. By bypassing some organizational challenges their existing culture posed and creating a relatively unfettered performance team in Boca Raton, IBM was able to enter the market expeditiously and own that space at least for a while. Ironically, some people point to IBM's later decision to reintegrate its PC business back into the parent corporation as the single biggest act that doomed its PC market primacy.

LOOKING BACK, THEN PUSHING FORWARD

The last decade, oft derided now that the bubble has deflated, still witnessed many examples of business agility. While others were trying to adapt to end-of-the-rainbow opportunities, agile companies were thoughtfully testing the waters and adapting to changes that had substance. While some companies were charging along to a drummer's beat they swore would never change, these agile companies varied their dance steps to their market's polyrhythms. As others built in haste, assuming ever-rising revenues would mask any waste, agile companies kept cutting fat and toning muscle, preferring best condition to first position.

As others built in haste, assuming ever-rising revenues would mask any waste, agile companies kept cutting fat and toning muscle, preferring best condition to first position.

When the downturn kicked in, many other companies reacted by cutting costs indiscriminately, but agile companies reflected and deliberated, making sensible reductions instead. While some company execs were hiding from suppliers, customers, media, and their own employees, agile company execs were taking confidence-building steps, reinforcing trust in their stakeholders. Where most saw one way, and that way seemed blocked, agile companies looked for and found alternative ways, preferring progress to "no-gress." And where others moved from fad to fad with scant follow-up evaluation, agile companies were fanatical about measuring the results of change and learning from what they found.

....

CHAPTER TWO

From the Top

As we wrote in the first chapter, the CEO is a critical part of developing and applying business agility. Without his or her wholehearted commitment, it is unlikely to take root. In later chapters we'll explore how, with CEO inspiration, companies can make use of agile business qualities to compete more effectively regardless of economic cycle phase. But before we do, it's important to consider how the board of directors, shareholders, suppliers, customers, and employees view the job and its responsibilities and how CEOs will be judged.

It is a gross understatement to say that business has changed immensely in the last half of the 20th century. The scope of competition, corporate structure, and business practice have all widened dramatically. At the same time, some things never change. Investors still hold boards and their CEOs responsible for delivering familiar financial results. The definitions of revenues and earnings have not changed, but their interrelationships with tangible and intangible assets certainly have. And so has the meaning of the qualitative term "shareholder value."

Never before has securities investing seen such rapid appreciation of share prices or such rapid loss. And not since the Great Depression has the veracity of financial reporting been viewed with as much suspicion. The term "transparent" means being able to see through something, and it may be no accident that the same term is used to describe clear, unambiguous, financial disclosure. The clamor for greater transparency is growing, and CEOs will be held ethically, if not legally, bound to deliver on it.

So, along with familiar and some new takes on financial results, CEOs will also be measured by a growing spate of non-financial issues.

BY WHAT MEASURES SHOULD THEY BE JUDGED?

Most will agree that it's hard to screw up in the midst of a boom. By the same token, a downturn typically presents one with choosing between lesser evils. CEOs often find themselves damned if they do and damned if they don't as they make their way through myriad tough decisions.

The problem, according to Rakesh Khurana of Harvard Business School, who has been studying the CEO issue, is that "We've made this a superhero job. Boards look at the CEO as

> **"We've made this a superhero job. Boards look at the CEO as a panacea and get fixated on the idea that one single individual will solve all of the company's problems."**
> **—Rakesh Khurana, Harvard Business School**

a panacea and get fixated on the idea that one single individual will solve all of the company's problems." The boom of the 1990s created a celebrity culture for CEOs. With the rise of the individual investor, the distance between corporate ivory tower and shareholder diminished. Formality became familiarity. It is only in recent times, after all, that entire companies, global *Fortune* 500 entities, have been symbolized by one-word monikers—Gates, Dell, Gerstner, Ellison....

The lionizing of the CEO began in the late 1970s and we might as well blame Lee Iacocca. His extraordinary turnaround of Chrysler, though funded in part by the government, was credited by some as near miraculous. So tightly interwoven is Iacocca's name with the Chrysler brand that it is hard to believe he ever worked anyplace else, much less that he actually built part of his career at rival carmaker Ford—coming to Chrysler only after being passed over for the top slot there.

A consummate marketer, Iacocca made Chrysler famous for such commercials as those that stated, "If you can find a better car, buy it." Such innovative tactics helped pull the company's slumping sales up sharply in the 1980s.

The success catapulted Iacocca into an icon of legendary status and, in all likelihood, made him the first CEO known by name to the ordinary rank and file American. His popularity soared so high that at one point he was seriously courted as a candidate for President of the United States.

In actuality, Khurana calls our recent phenomenon of mythologizing the CEO, the "leadership industrial complex."

By doing so, he suggests that in our thirst to continue to reap the rich windfall of the '90s boom and in our fear that such a boom might be short-lived, a certain "shamanism" has kicked in and boards, analysts, and the media have looked increasingly to the wizardry of an individual leader. Khurana suggests that in choosing CEOs, many boards have looked for known names, individuals who had been in the public eye and who had occupied many other top executive positions. More than seemingly any other characteristic, charisma was the most particular—and elusive—quality most sought by executive search teams.

Jeffrey Garten is currently a dean of the Yale School of Management, but his past life included 15 years on Wall Street as an investment banker and several others as a top official with the Commerce Department. He has channeled this unusual, some might say three-dimensional, experience of the CEO into a book, *The Mind of the CEO*. From this work, Garten has come away persuaded that "historians will conclude that the pressures of the era have proved much greater than anything most of these leaders could surmount. As a group, global CEOs will be seen as captains of small ships in turbulent seas—rarely able to chart a steady course and to maintain control of their own fate." He asserts that these men and women may rightly be viewed as captains of finance and industry, but not as supermen and women.

The mythologizing of the CEO has obscured the fact that major, multinational organizations are simply too large and too complex to be completely shaped by one person—particularly not in the short space of one to three years. The best executives, including Jack Welch, have always been deliberate in cultivating a support crew of deeply experienced mid- and senior-level leaders.

As McGraw-Hill's CEO, Harold W. (Terry) McGraw, pointed out when we interviewed him for this project, "The only thing a leader can really do is establish an environment in which progress can continue." Garry McGuire, the CFO of Avaya Communications, with whom we also spoke, echoed this statement, adding that the objective needs to be "giving goals and providing air cover."

> "The only thing a leader can really do is establish an environment in which progress can continue."
> —Terry McGraw, CEO, McGraw-Hill

McGraw's and McGuire's comments evoke a key point, namely that the businesses they are managing at the dawn of this new century are vastly more complex than any they would have managed during the setting of the last. Operating environments are much more competitive, business is conducted on a broader global field, and technology advancements have dramatically sped the pace and impact of events. Yet, in the face of such complexity, simplicity rules and there remains the tendency to stay reductionist when evaluating executive performance. As Anthony Bianco put it in his report for *Business Week*, it's "Get the stock price up. Period."

Warren Buffett, in the 1988 Berkshire Hathaway Annual Report, seemed rather cynical about CEO measurement. "The supreme irony of business management is that it is far easier for an inadequate CEO to keep his job than it is for an inadequate subordinate." In Buffett's view, an under-performing CEO could be "carried indefinitely" because "performance standards for his job seldom exist" and those that do are "often fuzzy or they may be waived or explained away...."

So, let's look at what the job entails. According to Steven Robbins, VentureCoach founder, writing for Expert.Zine, a CEO sets vision and strategy, builds culture, builds the senior management team, and allocates capital. These are certainly essential elements of developing business agility. But who grades the CEO? Ultimately, of course, it is the board that does so, and financial metrics rule for now.

Share Price

Shareholder pressures on companies to produce strong earnings and stock price appreciation are one of the reasons for the higher rates of churn in the top executive spot. Says John Challenger, "Companies today are under such pressure from Wall Street, quarter in and quarter out, that the bar keeps getting pushed higher. If companies don't hit these numbers, the CEO becomes a convenient scapegoat."

For the most part, share price fluctuation is unpredictable. And where some correlations of external events with price movement have been documented, the results are downright entertaining.

For example, a variety of studies have indicated the following. Prices have historically risen and fallen in lockstep with the average length of skirts in fashion. And prices have tended to rise following an NFC win in the Super Bowl and fall following an AFC win. From 1982 through 1997, stocks ran up an average annual gain of almost 25%, but when the skies were cloudy, stocks went up only a third as much. These patterns join such others as the month effect, where stocks tend to rise at the end and beginning of the month, and the weekend effect, where stocks tend to be lower on Mondays and higher on Fridays.

How often have you heard that a negative earning surprise by a well-known company in a sector has pulled down share prices for all the other companies in its sector? What if the problem wasn't lack of demand but poor cost control? It doesn't matter. Lots of investors simply shed shares in the sector. Positive earnings surprises can work the same way. Good news from a big sector "player" may pull up share prices for its competitors as well. But what if the good news was largely due to a major market-share shift? The big company's gain should logically accompany the competitor company's loss. But investor psychology does not always follow the logical course.

When a stock opens at $x and in 12 months rises to 60 times $x, "perfect market" adherents would still claim those prices are right. But what combination of magic, demand, and supply factors could make a company's market cap explode like that? Were the original IPO underwriters being way too conservative? The term "speculative bubble" sounds too tame to describe this phenomenon. It is nothing short of an investment riot—mob behavior. Should a CEO be held accountable for inciting this riot? Maybe not. And the mirror-image descent of share prices is also an extreme overreaction. Should the CEO be held accountable for that? Again, maybe not.

But, like it or not, CEOs will be held accountable. That's the job. It is the CEO's and management's responsibility to manage the expectations of its board, its analysts, and its investor community. This goes far beyond simply describing the outlook for the next quarter; it means taking these key constituents firmly into the fold to clearly (and frequently) explain the company's opportunities, capabilities, and actions. A CEO may not be able to prevent the mood swings of investor psychology, such as the seemingly irrational examples noted above, but with an educated and informed constituent network, a CEO will find his or her company much more accurately assessed.

A CEO may not be able to prevent the mood swings of investor psychology ... but with an educated and informed constituent network, a CEO will find his or her company much more accurately assessed.

Earnings

Agile executives also take a strong stance when it comes to earnings. The current lack of consistent standards over operating earnings and "pro forma" earnings has created a confusing setting for investors wherein different companies may pick and choose different categories of data to report.

Such differences in interpretation can make huge differences in calculated results. For example, a telecom network component's supplier wrote down its assets by $50 billion. Most of that write-down was based on goodwill impairment from a $41 billion acquisition that occurred at the peak of the dot.com bubble. These were losses stemming from stock transactions and for which no cash changed hands. Nevertheless, these charges were deducted from net income, creating a first-quarter loss that exceeded the company's previous five years of revenues by a factor of 10!

In its pro forma, the company excluded that $50 billion charge. Its rationale was these charges were about the past and meant nothing with regard to future business performance. That sounds reasonable, but "Not so fast," cautions Baruch Lev, professor of accounting at the Stern School of Business at New York University. With regard to instances like these, Lev asks, "Are these really one-time events? Or is this the beginning of an avalanche?" It's not easy to tell, but what is clear is that the interpretation of earnings in the absence of a standard makes things murky for investors and boards of directors.

> **By better defining, capturing, managing, and reporting on apt, business-focused performance data, these executives build value for their companies and in so doing Improve the quality of their own performance.**

Leading executives understand that it is in their own company's best interests to be as clear as possible in what they disclose and to disclose as fully as possible critical sources of value. In this way, agile leaders heed investors' desire for transparency by being forthright and clear about the measures they report. By better defining, capturing, managing, and reporting on apt, business-focused performance data, these executives build value for their companies and, in so doing, improve the quality of their own performance.

A Two-Way Street

Boards of directors also have a responsibility to let go of some residual expectations remaining from the protracted growth phase of the economy. Double-digit growth, year to year, may be possible in some industries but impossible in others. Setting that as an expectation for all companies and CEOs is a recipe for failure and continued disappointment.

Jack Welch has said he expects his successor, Jeffrey Immelt, to run GE for another 20 years. But if GE's board expects him to perform the same feats as Jack, he won't last. To his credit, Welch wrung a lot of costs out of the GE he inherited. It had some fat and Welch made it lean. Immelt inherited a lean GE. There's the danger that an expectation of big cost savings may remove muscle mass this time around.

THE NEED TO DEFINE SHAREHOLDER VALUE

One of the measures for which CEOs are held accountable is *shareholder value*. Left to their own devices, shareholders will define for themselves what shareholder value means. So, it is important for CEOs to describe how they define shareholder value. The idea is not to convince everyone to change their definitions; it is to inform everyone how the CEO views things and what measures he or she will seek to improve.

It is easy to argue that book value, dissolution value, and market capitalization do not represent the "true" value of a company. Book value often doesn't include intangible assets that are sometimes more significant than tangible assets in generating revenues and making profits. Dissolution value also often ignores intangibles plus any value adds provided by how the various pieces once worked together. Market capitalization's volatility augurs against its reliability, too.

One could simply say there's no precise, indisputable way to assign a worth figure to publicly traded companies. By default, then, we're back to the notion that they're worth whatever someone is willing to pay for them. And that takes us back to market capitalization—the continual recalculation of share price multiplied by shares outstanding—because that represents what the shareholders collectively are willing to pay for those companies at any moment. As such, we need to understand why they buy one company's stock instead of another's.

The institutional investor may analyze results for the last five years, do a forward analysis based on similar performance, compare one company's performance with the sector's performance, and conclude that the stock represents a fair price. As for the individual investors, they have other reasons. A broker may recommend the stock. They may have overheard someone saying the stock was undervalued. They may have read an article about the company in *Business Week* and liked what they read. They may subscribe to an investor newsletter that picked the stock as a good buy.

The institutional investors and savvy individual investors tend to be value investors. They are looking for long-term positions with companies whose shares they believe are underpriced relative to future performance prospects. Many have a Warren Buffett-like obsession with the quality of management. And these are the investors whose decisions to buy or sell your shares will cause those prices to move, significantly. You want these investors on your side. You want to know their definition of shareholder value and you want them to know yours.

Many of them have bought into the formal concept of shareholder value and the two closely associated measurement approaches: shareholder value analysis (SVA) and economic value added (EVA). They're looking at "the net present value of a company's future cash flows discounted at the appropriate cost of capital." They believe these measurements are more meaningful than profitability, because it's easy to manipulate profitability figures over the short term by moving items onto or off the balance sheet. And they believe it gives them a leg up on earnings-per-share, because that metric does not reflect the asset investment needed to achieve those earnings.

The use of discounted cash flows as a metric addresses the criticism of the backward-looking nature of earnings-per-share, current assets, and other more mainstream metrics. Value creation, its proponents believe, must take a long-term point of view, manage all cash flows on both the income statement and the balance sheet, and understand how to compare cash flows from different time periods on a risk-adjusted basis. It is by definition a long-term view of future prospects.

CEOs who adhere to SVA can point to several value drivers as factors to concentrate on and areas by which their performance can be measured. If a CEO and/or management have created their own hybrid definition of shareholder value, they can identify their own set of drivers and take care to communicate them. In either case, management is being proactive. They are establishing and discussing the performance measures they will use and can help guide others in making meaningful assessments.

Not all measures will be financial. These days, especially, many non-financial qualities are being scrutinized. There was a time when people expected very different things from the public and private sectors. Few expected government agencies to be efficient or cost-conscious, and even fewer expected corporations to worry about environmental concerns. How things have changed.

AUTHENTICITY AND TRUST

In the book, *Security Transformation*, the authors talked about the critical part trust plays in all business dealings and transactions. In the wake of recent business scandals, trust has become far more precious. Along with financial results, CEOs will be expected to be who they say they are and do what they say they'll do. Their word will either cement the performance team's commitment or, if suspect, lead to its undoing. Trust is a valuable coin, but worthless if misspent.

Trust is a valuable coin, but worthless if misspent.

This excerpt from a paper by Ivy Sea Online really gets to the heart of being what you say you are:

So to be a truly genuine—or authentic—leader requires a few things: To ensure one's corporate actions and rhetoric are aligned; to ensure that such actions are meaningful (as opposed to superficial, headline-grabbing actions that don't permeate or take root beyond the organization's need for disingenuous publicity); and to ensure that one's public persona and private core are not at odds. And we wonder why it's so lonely at the proverbial "top," or why truly authentic leadership is a rarity.... It's not so easy to get an organization that has assumed a life of its own, driven more and more by the insatiable appetite of shareholder value, to actually be that ideal. The proof is in the follow-through. That's where the level of leadership commitment and influence becomes, often painfully, evident.

Eileen McDargh, a corporate consultant specializing in "uncovering soul in the workplace," offers these observations:

Is there congruency between what is said and what is practiced? Are people invited to participate and then ignored when they do? Does the organization preach empowerment but then require multiple sign-offs before action takes place? Do managers claim to have an open-door policy but then respond in anger when they hear something they don't like? These are just some of the questions which, when honestly answered, can indicate if there's breathing space for the soul. Engaging the human spirit is the softer side of business. But without the "software" of soul/spirit, you'll never truly engage the mindware. And that's what ultimately creates the competitive edge for the future.

That's what helps increase business agility.

GOOD CORPORATE CITIZENSHIP

Good corporate citizenship is good business, simple as that. Businesses that are active in charitable and community causes receive an associative positive brand effect. This allows a company to be perceived more favorably in the community. In addition, studies have shown that employees prefer to work for companies whose values are aligned with theirs, companies with character, companies perceived as "good." This is one of the reasons why so many businesses invest hugely in such annual "best places to work" applications, such as the influential *Working Mothers* magazine ranking. Other leading companies make a point of deeply embedding community values into their corporate culture, like the following story of Applied Materials.

> Good corporate citizenship is good business, simple as that. Businesses that are active in charitable and community causes receive an associative positive brand effect.

Applied Materials

In California's Silicon Valley, in the early '90s, unemployment was rising, real estate occupancy was falling, and the Valley's political, civic, and business communities were at war with one another.

The San Jose Silicon Valley Chamber of Commerce proposed a new organization to bring big business and the community together. But conspicuously missing were the big, high-tech businesses. They were all so busy paying attention to matters elsewhere that they seemed to be removed from the problems in their communities.

Jim Morgan, CEO of Applied Materials, stepped up to bat, though. He personally lobbied his fellow CEOs and in 1992 helped create Joint Venture Silicon Valley, a coalition of business, government, and community members.

At first, Joint Venture tackled practical business obstacles. Thanks to its efforts, 27 cities and two counties adopted a uniform building code, streamlining the building permit process for growing companies and ensuring new job creation. Then Joint Venture turned its sights on education. Substandard public schools were putting Valley companies at a disadvantage. The group raised millions for teachers to set standards for math, science, and other subjects. And they came up with ways to help students meet those standards, to pay teachers to work extra hours, and to provide computer hardware. Joint Venture Silicon Valley provided mentors and set up programs to train teachers in multimedia technology. Now, it is tackling the digital divide.

Companies like Applied tweak the nose of cynics who may feel that corporate interests outweigh all others. Applied's contribution and those of like-minded companies are based on a fundamental belief that they, who have benefited so greatly from their community, have an obligation to give back. They are also based on a fundamental pragmatism. Raising economic and educational parity in turn increases the brain pool that global competitors can draw from. This will ultimately help to mitigate the human resource war for scarce, highly trained talent.

ENVIRONMENTAL AND SOCIAL CONCERNS

Environmental and social concerns, once considered soft issues, are increasingly being added to the CEO's plate of responsibilities. This is particularly true in Europe, where the public, investors, governments, and businesses are expanding the notion of corporate leadership to include not only out-standing economic perform-ance, but also exemplary achievement in environmental, ethical, and social matters. Businesses that embrace these concerns understand that issues such as resource depletion, global warming, poor labor conditions, anti-competitive trade practices, and corruption clearly serve to erode stakeholder confidence.

> Environmental and social concerns, once considered soft issues, are increasingly being added to the CEO's plate of responsibilities.

Nike, the American footwear company, was put off stride when revelations of substandard factory conditions in Asia and the Caribbean were made public. Ensuing boycotts and damaging press reports sullied the shoe company's brand and cost it heavily both financially and in terms of strategic momentum.

The issues surrounding the collapse of Enron Corporation will likely place increasing scrutiny on the ethical practices of other companies. Agile executives will work proactively to ensure that their business practices and methods are beyond reproach. These leading companies will find new ways to dis-tinguish their reputation and integrate environmental and social management and shareholder interests into their core communication and core business activities in order to improve their business performance. The benefits of doing so include reputation and brand enhancement, evidence of good corporate citizenship, and recruitment and retention of excellent people.

EVIDENCE OF AGILITY

Earlier, we described the qualities that underlie business agility. Here, we describe the characteristics we have observed of agility in action.

Creative

Creative can be an overused word. And the expression "out of the box" risks becoming hackneyed. But that's what it takes to solve seemingly insolvable problems. Thomas Ryder, CEO of *Reader's Digest*, says the media industry's preoccupation with advertising revenue shortfalls is missing the real iceberg. "Subscriptions is where the real problem lies," he revealed. Magazine publishers, Ryder told us, have done a great job of training consumers to expect low subscription prices. "Some are so low," he laughed, "that they fail to cover the cost of ink and paper."

But it's the cost of delivery and the cost of sales that are really taking a toll. And unlike advertising, which is historically cyclical, these costs appear to be relentlessly increasing. "About 90 million subscriptions were sold through a couple of third parties," such as Publishers Clearing House (the group that sent those letters offering big prizes in its annual lottery). Today, said Ryder, these groups are all but defunct and, so far, alternative sales strategies are not making up for the shortfall. In addition, the mailing costs for magazines keep tracking the increases in U.S. postal rates.

> "We may end up literally delivering the magazines to the postal delivery person on his or her route, paying less for the postage, and saving significant costs."
> —Tom Ryder, CEO, Reader's Digest.

Solving these problems, Ryder offered, would take some thinking out of the box. For example, "publishers may have to take on a significant portion of postal service tasks, particularly the 'last mile' responsibilities." Instead of sending magazines from the printer, through the mails, to subscribers, "we may end up literally delivering the magazines to the postal delivery person on his or her route, paying less for the postage, and saving significant costs." Now, that's creative.

Culture

Corporations do have distinct cultures, even when they are in the same business. Walk into a Wal-Mart store, browse around a while, and then do the same at its competitors. You'll experience cultural diversification firsthand. The "greeter" at the front of Wal-Mart may seem corny to some, but that customer-centric culture permeates all Wal-Mart stores. It's no accident that Wal-Mart was able to motivate its "associates" to cut inventory when sales began to slacken. And it ended up with a very profitable fourth-quarter 2001 result while many other retailers were faltering.

"A performance culture is in great part picking the right people and letting them go forward," offered McGraw. We'll take a more in depth look at performance culture in chapter five.

Communications

The time when most CEOs would prefer not to communicate is the very time when they need to do it most. Not every CEO conveys the inspirational "juice" of an Iacocca, but they don't have to. What investors, customers, suppliers, and employees want most is "no surprises." People can handle bad news; it's no news that they hate.

For Carl Vogel, CEO of Charter Communications, looking at successes and the lack thereof, it comes down to delivering a message that people can understand and a clearly communicated goal that they can see. "It sounds simple," he says, "but if you communicate well with people and keep your employees motivated and positive, they'll be with you through the ups and downs."

In chapter four, we'll see how CEOs use internal and external communications to effectively manage morale, support key corporate and market strategies, keep editors and analysts informed, and enhance corporate and product brand management.

Cost-Consciousness

Effective cost management must be an ingrained aspect of your business. It's not something you roll out when sales are slowing and put away when sales are building; it needs to be a continuous process. "It takes waste out of the system at all times, and improves results at all times," said Ryder.

What is often overlooked, however, is that innovation and creativity can be applied with the same discipline to the areas of cost management as they can to product innovation and development, with excellent and often unexpected results. The old rule about cost elimination is that the options are formulaic and finite (cut headcount, implement furloughs, trim budgets by 10%, etc). The reality is far different. Chapter seven examines creative alternatives for optimal cost management with minimal negative impact on competitiveness and morale.

Consistency

When the mob rules and speculators prowl, the people are betting on long shots, not favorites. But it's the CEO's job to remind everyone that consistency does pay off. It pays off in profitability, sustainability, and less volatility. One may not see hyper-growing share prices, but one won't see fast-shrinking ones, either.

Look at GE. It's categorized as a conglomerate, but unlike conglomerates of old, there is a rationale for all its businesses, and there is a sharing of knowledge—cross-pollination—that permeates the culture. And it is consistent, delivering revenues, delivering profits, delivering real, sustainable growth.

There's no overarching technique for delivering consistent results. Chapter nine looks at ways of identifying new value without requiring wholesale changes in business models and practices.

GETTING REAL

The downturn of 2000 and the recession of 2001 have given the market a dose of reality. The virtually interest-free financing of ever-rising share prices is gone. So, too, is supply chasing unbridled demand.

It's time for CEOs to acknowledge that huge share price ups and downs reflect neither the real potentials nor the pitfalls of their businesses. What counts is consistency and communication. What matters is the speed and accuracy of continuous market assessment and the ability to adapt to changes quickly.

CHAPTER THREE

Challenging Conventional Wisdom

They say a failure to study the lessons of history dooms us to repeat them. In retrospect, the heady years of 1998 and 1999 are full of lessons. It was no accident that we got where we were in 1999 or, for that matter, 2001. There is even logic beneath some of the illogic that permeated strategies and tactics now held in contempt.

It is no cliché to say we were plowing new ground. The sudden confluence of fast and ubiquitous connectivity with huge volumes of time-sensitive data fed our most far-fetched optimism. We were philosophically prepared to "boldly go where no man had gone before." And we thought we had the foolproof means of getting there.

Time-tested rules were rewritten or ignored. Economic cycles that had recurred faithfully for centuries, like the phases of our moon, were now challenged by the ingenuity of man and our hubris. Like a pendulum, we swung from deliberative, facts-based decision making to frenzied wagers based on whims. And, now as the pendulum has swung back to level-headedness, we run the risk of painting all aspects of our "folly" with the same brush of dismissal. And that's a mistake.

We need to revisit how things played out, rid ourselves of notions that proved to be erroneous, and hold tightly to those that showed unshakeable validity. Here, we will rewind the tape and see that the events of 1999 through 2001 were neither random nor accidental. Then, we'll look at strategies once held in high regard and now stamped "bogus." We'll also take a look at the debate over structural productivity to see what our prospects may be limited to as we go forward.

A LOOK BACK

During rough times, we tend to look back. Some of us do it wistfully; others do it in an attempt to understand what happened and why. During the expansion, many of us unquestioningly adopted new precepts about market entry speed and business performance. Clearly, Web mania had its part in how we got here. But it needs to be looked at in the context of where we were. Without the conditions that prevailed leading up to the dot.com bubble, and their impact on management from a business model and execution standpoint, the bubble would not have happened.

The early 1990s were the beginning of a decade-long economic expansion. We were growing again, continuing to innovate, and reaping the rewards that come from increasing productivity. And we were exploring. Management consulting introduced us to business reengineering, and many of us forged ahead trying to increase efficiency, cut costs, and increase profits. Information technology continued to offer us more and novel ways to squeeze communication latency, collect and analyze information, and integrate our efforts in more coordinated ways.

Local area networks showed us the value of intra-company electronic mail and shared databases. The new administration in Washington talked about "information highways." Our expanding global economy was increasing our personal incomes and our companies' incomes. By the time the Web and Web browsers were ready for prime time, the economy was primed to embrace them. We were ready for the next "new" thing, and many of us believed it had arrived. Our confidence in our economy and our businesses was growing even as our aversion to risk was waning. So, we were predisposed to the suspension of disbelief as we first contemplated "the Net." We were ready to adopt a new religion along with its new lexicon and driving principles. And so we did.

Relatively obscure for its first two decades, the Internet and its World Wide Web seemed to be everywhere, doing everything by 1996. We could get our news from the Web, buy things off the Web, play games on the Web, and earn our degrees through the Web. We could buy cars and insurance, find jobs, do our banking, and do all vacation planning, plane ticket buying, plus hotel and car reserving using the Web. By golly, once they put all those "fiber-whatsits" in place, we could be listening to music and watching movies on the Web, too. And what about free long-distance calls using the Web?

What existing industries didn't feel both exhilarated and threatened by these prospects? The Web was the ultimate disruptive technology, promising to lay waste to the old companies and old ways of thinking while offering a bountiful harvest to those who took it to heart. Amazon was putting the fear of God into Barnes and Noble. E*Trade had the full-service brokerages quaking in their boots. Double-Click was dominating the online advertising space even as Madison Avenue was trying to figure out what a banner ad was.

> **The Web was the ultimate disruptive technology, promising to lay waste to the old companies and old ways of thinking while offering a bountiful harvest to those who took it to heart.**

Publications companies that made their livings selling subscriptions and advertising space in products they printed bemoaned a time when readers would scroll instead of flip pages. And with Web sites dedicated to searching and comparing prices of insurance offerings, insurance companies worried about what effect that would have on the margins they earned through consumers' price ignorance.

It looked like this new "e" thing would blow up all the infrastructures so carefully constructed over the last century and change all the rules in its wake. The seeming suddenness of its appearance and pervasive prospects for change over so wide a swath made the Web a tantalizing enigma for investors, analysts, and CEOs.

With the exception of a few people, everyone seemed at

equal loss to predict exactly how the Web would wend its way through everything we do, but most accepted the inevitability of it all. So, in our fear and amazement, we looked for those few who were said to "get it." We sat at their feet, listening wide-eyed, as they got increasingly animated, pacing, drawing charts, talking about "hits" and disintermediation, and painting verbal and graphic pictures of the coming brave new world.

It was a world where things happened so fast—"at Internet speed"—that those who deliberated would be losers. It was a world where things like short-term profitability, cost-consciousness, economic cycles, and planning were disparaged in favor of things like first-mover status and click-speed decisions.

Everyone wanted to "get it." Getting it was hip. It elevated the geek into a tycoon, the acne-faced teenager into an online wheeler-dealer, the enlightened CEO into a demigod. Our language was filling with new marketing acronyms—B2B, B2C, C2C. And the wallets of those who got it seemed to be getting fatter at Internet speed. Bricks-and-mortar was passé; clicks-and-order was *de rigueur*.

Market analysts wrote volumes about Web strategies. Business reporters jumped up at news conferences and shouted questions about Web strategies. Hewlett-Packard held an event at the upscale Fairmont Hotel in San Jose, California, invited 5,000 dignitaries from around the world, and held a half-day multimedia extravaganza to announce its Web strategy. Web strategies were big news. Not having a Web strategy was cause for alarm, even if you were a wholesale plumbing distribution company in Sheboygan, Wisconsin.

In all that noise, all that excitement, there were more than a few investors, analysts, and CEOs questioning where the Web facts left off and hype began. They had logic and history firmly on their side, but the Web had "buzz" and religious-like fervor on its side. Who could argue with dot.com IPOs and their meteoric price run-ups? We had suspended disbelief. And buzz won.

Historically, every speculative bubble has been preceded by a period of rational investment and business growth. Somewhere, though, a line is crossed and the prevailing behavior changes from rational to irrational, from logical to illogical, from skeptical to gullible. Afterward, we swing back toward excessive caution. In the past, speculative bubbles have certainly affected the securities markets, but had minimal direct effect on business markets. This bubble has been an exception. Some of the irrational, illogical, and gullible behavior snuck into the business market, too.

> **Somewhere, though, a line is crossed and the prevailing behavior changes from rational to irrational, from logical to illogical, from skeptical to gullible.**

A RECESSION-PROOF ECONOMY

We were ready to believe that our new economy—bolstered by an unimaginable confluence of innovative information technology and ubiquitous connectivity—was changing the natural laws of economics and recessions were now history.

Long before anyone considered studying economics, there were economic cycles. Economic cycles appeared to be intrinsic to trade. We all understand what underlies expansions, recessions, and the periods in between. And we understand what happens to things like employment, prices, inventories, profits, and interest rates during the various phases of an economic cycle.

But we were also given to believe that a fundamental cause of recessions was the periodic mismatch of supply and demand forces. Therefore, it stood to reason that if new technologies could mitigate these mismatches, the results would be mitigated too. Instead of the probability of widely oscillating ups and downs, there was the very real possibility of highly damped ups and downs. Hence, we have the prospect of a recession-proof economy—a "new economy."

A system of advanced IT technologies blended with the Internet's penchant for integration and information dissemination could crank up or crank down production in sync with fluctuations in demand. Because such a system could do the job in near real time, and work with smaller demand batches, it seemed reasonable to expect that supply/demand mismatches could never get very big.

Some experts reasoned it might never take more than two quarters of crank-down to bring things back in line. So, contractions were still possible, but recessions (two quarters of back-to-back negative growth) could become extinct. These advanced technologies coupled with complementary control techniques would tame those periodic economic waves into predictable, controllable, good vibrations.

On the face of it, a recession would mean all bets are off. Any claim of recession resistance would seem baseless. But that judgment may be hasty. What if the pilots rather than the plane were at fault? What if the system was working just fine, but dot.com suppliers were making egregious risk-management errors?

Regardless of what system one uses, prudent business assigns risks to demand based on its source. An order from a company that has been manufacturing products, profitably, for five years has less risk associated with it than one from a new company with no track record. The possibility of not being paid or cancellation of the order is much higher with the second than with the first company. Risk management requires different handling of those two orders. And, if done appropriately, the risk can be mitigated and there's less chance of exposure.

Had all demand been appropriately risk-managed, there's a very real possibility that the "new economy" would have been more recession-resistant. But that's not what happened. The dot.com bubble produced a flurry of new, cash-rich companies that seemed to be spending equally on technology products and "image" promotion. In aggregate, the demand represented by these companies was large

> **Had all demand been appropriately risk-managed, there's a very real possibility that the "new economy" would have been more recession-resistant.**

enough to set off a crank-up in production. Their market caps at the bubble's peak gave them lots of credit cachet. If companies treated their new customers as low-risk demand sources and financed their demand, it would tend to accelerate production spending, spurring more hiring and capacity expansion, without triggering the risk-management safety devices that hedge against order cancellation or non-payment.

If, on the other hand, companies had treated dot.com demand as higher-risk orders, risk-management safety valves would have opened. The share price crash would still have set off a chain reaction of order cancellations and inability to pay for products ordered and delivered, but the companies that had risk-managed those orders might have been far less damaged.

There are many reasons why otherwise prudent companies may have chosen to overlook the heightened risk of dot.com demand. The business-model track records were non-existent, but dot.coms proved they could raise money. Sales competition was fierce, so playing hardball on credit could have doomed some transactions. And some of us had simply gotten Web religion. Anirvan Banerji, with the Economic Cycle Research Institute in New York, said, "The crowning irony of the return of the business-cycle recession is that it was triggered precisely by the misperceptions of risk that led to the unsustainable excesses of the cycle."

Had risk-management been applied extensively to dot.com demand, it would not have prevented an economic contraction. There would still have been that shift from mania to depression that happens at the end of every speculative bubble. There would still have been the rapid crash of dot.com market caps. It would still have spawned widespread order cancellation and bankruptcy proceedings. But it could have mitigated supplier losses, reduced inventory overhang, and made us all look a little less irrational, illogical, and gullible.

REVISED LESSONS

As the economy expanded and the dot.com bubble began emerging, new rules of competitive engagement started taking hold. Terms like "first-mover advantage" and "customer-driven" were used so loosely and so often that their meanings became smears of definitions. Every dot.com startup resurrected the early concept of first-mover advantage and made it a primary business-plan objective. Most new products or services were described as customer-driven. Most companies and business decisions were described as moving at Internet speed. The winners were those who seized the moment. Make it happen now and get it right later.

> **Terms like "first-mover advantage" and "customer-driven" were used so loosely and so often that their meanings became smears of definitions**

Being Best Is More Important Than Being First

What exactly is the advantage gained by moving first? And which customers are we talking about who keep driving new products and services? In the absence of deliberation, or at least a thoughtful discussion, the meanings of these terms are expansive. If a company is trying to raise capital and cites "first-mover advantage" as a key investment factor, what are potential investors to make of that claim? And should all customers be equally influential in your determination of product/service features and benefits?

It's not really clear what led to all the hyperbole about being first out with a new product or service category. But for a while, anyway, it was definitely the expression *du jour*. Analysts and business news reporters really seemed to grab onto it. Merrill Lynch analyst Jonathan Cohen wrote in January 1999, Inktomi "can benefit substantially from its first-mover advantage." In December 1998, *Business Week* wrote a complimentary Amazon profile describing its "crucial first-mover advantage." And the *Wall Street Corporate Reporter* quoted DoubleClick CEO, Kevin O'Connor, as calling "first-mover advantage" one of the company's "three huge advantages over the competition."

People even gave it a value. Phil Leigh, vice president at Raymond James Financial in St. Petersburg, Florida, said first-mover advantage was worth a 100% to 150% premium over how a stock might be valued using other measures. And we guess it still has some residual cachet, as witnessed by this headline from a Nortel press release from January 2001: "Nortel Networks Grows First-Mover Advantage in China's Local Internet Market."

Maybe the perception stems from the rush by homesteaders to be first in a new territory and plant their stakes on the choicest piece of ground. Or maybe it's a misinterpretation of the benefits of being a market leader (e.g., higher margins, lower cost of sales, etc.). In any case, the evidence for a cascade of benefits accruing from being first in a market is pretty thin, and the evidence for it not being such a big deal is a lot thicker.

That said, where there is little opportunity for either product or service differentiation, being first to the market is an advantage. Amazon.com did nothing different from Borders.com or BarnesandNoble.com. It simply did it first and developed an impressive customer base before the other two got their acts together. The same could be said about UPS's online shipping and

Where there can be significant differentiation, being first can be a disadvantage.

tracking following on the heels of FedEx. But where there can be significant differentiation, being first can be a disadvantage.

Take for example personal digital assistants (PDAs). The first mover was Apple with Newton. Currently, the winner is Palm. In VCRs, Sony's Betamax machine paved the way and was run over by Matsushita's (and several other companies') VHS recorders. Sun's engineering workstations were a distant second to Apollo's. And White Castle fast-food hamburgers were decades ahead of Ray Kroc's McDonald's. In fact, Henry Ford was reputed to have quipped, "The best strategy is to be the first person to be second."

There clearly are some advantages to being first to do something. And there are also many risks. Some advantages are: no immediate, direct competitors; a perception of ingenuity and/or novelty; and the opportunity to define product/service features. Some risks are: the secret's out before the market begins to adopt; you bear all the market education costs; and you have to overcome the market's credibility hurdles.

If you identified, enumerated, and gave relative weight to all the advantages and risks, the odds are the risks would outweigh the advantages in most cases. This is not to say you should avoid being first; it is simply to say that any advantages you might gain will be accompanied by a bunch of risks.

The value of having identified and quantified these risks is it gives you the opportunity to hedge many of them without necessarily giving up the first-mover position. For example, you could do it as a coordinated effort with companies likely to provide ancillary products and services. They would share some of the market-education costs and lend credibility to the market launch. You would still be first to market, but potential customers would see more of the whole-product visage.

Here's an apt example. In the early 1980s after IBM had introduced its first PC, Apple unveiled its Lisa computer. Lisa made Apple a first mover in personal computers that have a graphical user interface. The product was big, it was expensive (e.g., about $10,000), it had no provisions for expansion, and no software vendors had written applications for it, yet. But it was incredibly innovative and much easier to use than the IBM DOS-based machine. It came out after *Time* magazine featured a personal computer as its "man of the year," when a mini-bubble was emerging around PC-oriented stocks. But despite the market's predisposition to accept it, the Lisa was a significant failure. The market was looking for expandability and Lisa had none. It was looking for a choice in basic productivity software. Again, there was none.

Two years later, when Apple was poised to announce the first affordable graphical-user-interface computer (Macintosh), the market had become far more skeptical. Several PC clone companies had suffered huge losses and PC sales were way off projections. Had Apple gone it alone, again, the result most likely would have been the same—or worse. But they learned from Lisa. The Macintosh was launched in conjunction with news about significant orders from noteworthy universities. It was also accompanied by announcements of key personal productivity software applications and printers that could match its graphics-oriented bent. So, despite the negative market environment, the Apple Macintosh became a market success. Apple still got first-mover credit, but this time it had managed the associated risks.

The moral of this story is first-mover status is no guarantee of success. In fact, most first movers do not end up being leaders. But, there are ways to retain many first-mover benefits while reducing some first-mover risks. In the end, the glory may end up being shared, but so are the costs and uncertainties.

Segmenting the Customers Who Drive Your Business— Profitability over Market Share

In the hoopla surrounding the "customer is king" excitement, companies often described themselves as "customer-driven," implying all customers. And maybe that made sense in the mad rush to expand at all costs during the "boom." But market share for market share's sake is false logic for the simple reason that all customers are not equal. All customers will not spend as much with you over time. The goal must necessarily center on profitability. So, at a time when the focus is optimizing the revenue per customer, spending equal amounts on all customers

Market share for market share's sake is false logic for the simple reason that all customers are not equal.

makes little business sense. Some customers are more important to your business, and you need to be able to identify and group them. But deciding how to segment your customers and how to apportion what you spend on them is not a technology issue.

There is no shortage of technologies aimed at customer relationship management (CRM) and customer segmentation. The problem is we rely too much on the tools, and the best tools are only as good as the hand that wields them. As the old joke about the IBM repairman who used only a hammer puts it, "It's not hitting with the hammer, it's knowing where to hit." The same goes for customer segmentation. The systems will do the slicing and dicing for us but we need to tell them where to cut. And that's easier said than done.

Telecom companies have been known to offer bonuses to customers who are most likely to "churn," while ignoring customers who are more steadfast in their loyalty. Many companies spend far more (about 10 times more) soliciting new customers than they do preserving and nurturing existing customer relationships. Most companies consider a 3% response to direct mail solicitation a very good return. But with a mass mailing to 100,000 people, at a cost of $150,000, a response by 3,000 means the cost per response is $50. If 30,000 people respond, the cost goes down to $5. And some companies are getting 30% response. The difference is often a consequence of how they segment their customers.

There is no customer-segmentation "machine." It is a process involving multiple people and systems. We have to be able to gather and consolidate information from a variety of systems, some of which may be integrated, others of which may be standalone. We need experts in statistics and programming to put together the algorithms that can hash through tons of data to sort customers into segments. Marketing and IT departments have to work together to decide what data to gather in the first place. And the whole complex infrastructure for gathering, storing, processing, and distributing information has to be accessible and robust.

But even before you get to the problem of constructing a customer-segmentation solution, you need "to understand why you're segmenting your customers a certain way and why that way makes sense for your business," said Barbara Bund, a senior lecturer at MIT's Sloan School of Management. Bund used the consumer electronics industry as an example. Consumer electronic companies tend to segment their customers by age and income, but Bund doesn't think that kind of data has much relationship to customer buying patterns. Instead, she suggested, they should divide customers by technology comfort. But that is not usually a question on a registration form's mini-marketing survey.

Banks and cable TV operators note that customers who buy packages of services tend to be less prone to switching to other banks or direct broadcast satellite alternatives. But what is the correlation between other demographic profile data and propensity to purchase packaged services? Is it age? Is it income? Is it gender? Is it education? When analysts find combinations of profile data that correlate to a desired behavior, they can create a segment and populate it with customers that fit that profile. And when they really "nail it," that's what helps to garner those 20% to 30% responses.

Most PC companies sell products in two basic form factors—desktops and laptops. They could segment their customers into those who own desktops and those who own laptops, then target desktop-specific accessories to the first segment and laptop-specific ones to the second segment. But they could also create segments based on how the products are used, such as those who use them for work and those who use them at home. Here, again, accessories could be grouped by likely work versus home computer need and marketed to the appropriate segment. The better the match between a product's application and a segment's implicit need for that application, the greater the potential for finer targeting and greater marketing efficiency.

The better the match between a product's application and a segment's implicit need for that application, the greater the potential for finer targeting and greater marketing efficiency.

But what do you do when the data you're looking for is not data that has been specifically captured? Company ABC sells both consumer electronic items and computer-related accessories. A new product it plans to introduce (a wireless network hub for small office and sophisticated home users) would definitely appeal to some small office and home office customers, but not all.

Customers having only one computer may need it for Internet access portability. A laptop equipped with a wireless network interface card could be moved from room to room while still having access to the Web. Customers having multiple systems might use it to avoid having to run a wired network and having to modify the wiring as space is rearranged. In any case, installing the product requires some technical know-how and the user's manual is not user friendly.

Nowhere in the database is there a field for technical aversion or technical affinity. But there are fields for the different kinds of equipment customers already have, for the kinds of applications they plan to use on their computers, and so on. One could create a profile of customers that shows which customers have Internet access and which have business-oriented systems and accessories. In addition, accessories can be weighted as to the technical knowledge required to install them. A new segment can be created using all of these criteria to carve out a list of names from the customer database. A pilot campaign can be tried first to sample response and, if it looks good, a larger campaign can be launched to that segment. When ABC sent out direct mail pieces to its entire customer database, the response was less than 2%, and half of that response was for further information. When they customized a segment using the above criteria, the response was nearly 15%, and 60% were orders for the wireless hub.

Particularly during an economic contraction, when spending is curtailed, every company should be combing through its customer databases and segmenting them in ways that might reduce the overall cost of sales and increase the most profitable revenues.

It's Need, Not Speed!

During the heat of the dot.com speculative bubble, there was far too much emphasis on acting "at Internet speed." One victim of this collective race to act quickly has been value-proposition clarity. To be sure, even in less frantic times many companies have had problems stating cogent value propositions. But haste exacerbates the situation.

Whether in the midst of expansion, recession, or somewhere in between, there's a constant battle over reflective versus reflexive action. It wasn't very long ago that leading companies were talking about "business reflexes," strongly implying that speed of action was more important than exploring any underlying need for action. We saw venture capitalists backing three competitors to avoid the possibility of backing the wrong one or losing the opportunity because of deliberation hesitation. The prevailing strategy appeared to be act now and worry about it later.

> **It wasn't very long ago that leading companies were talking about "business reflexes," strongly implying that speed of action was more important than exploring any underlying need for action.**

There was also a double standard in place regarding risk management. Companies still hedged foreign currency fluctuations and made sure they were adequately insured against natural disasters. But as we pointed out earlier, many companies let down their guard in assessing the risk associated with dot.com demand. And few companies used risk as a way to evaluate opportunities and adjust priorities.

With all the push to be fast, to be first, to be fearless, most of the "innovations" described by new business and new venture plans were more variations on an existing theme than truly novel ideas. Many depended heavily on new behaviors by Internet users without the compelling benefits needed to accomplish those behavior modifications.

"Just do it," says the Nike slogan. "Being faster is everything," says one market guru. "You don't have the time to get it perfect, so don't bother trying," advises another. Which raises the question, is it better to act fast or act smart? In physiology, reflex by definition is action that occurs before the brain can process the stimulus. It is the quick response of the eye's pupil to bright light, the flexing of the calf muscle to a blow just below the knee. Reflexive action is fast, not decisive. Decisive means consideration has taken place.

There was nothing fast in how eBay began or how it has innovated over time. None of the founders had today's eBay reality as their driving vision. In fact, Pierre Omidyar created an auction site for Pez dispenser collectors. Today's eBay grew through deliberative, incremental changes and still grows that way. At one point, Meg Whitman, eBay's CEO, had to decide whether to continue charging commissions on auction sales or adopt a free auction service such as Yahoo!

was preparing to launch. "Free is usually a pretty good proposition," Whitman observed stoically, but after deliberating the advantages and disadvantages, Whitman chose to stick with the original model and retain the fees. Yahoo! launched its free auction service and some potential eBay users opted for the free service. But eBay's community continued to grow much faster than any other auction site's, and Whitman's decision was vindicated when Yahoo! Auctions began charging for its listings, too.

David Filo and Jerry Yang were Ph.D. candidates in electrical engineering at Stanford University. Yahoo! is a direct outgrowth of their own interests in various Internet subjects and their casual efforts at categorizing and subcategorizing in order to build a more user-friendly Internet guide. Their Web site started out as "Jerry's Guide to the World Wide Web," and it also grew through deliberative, incremental changes plus a lot of word-of-mouth. It took 10 months from when they started their Web guide before they had racked up a one-million-hit day. And it was only after the interest and hit rates continued to grow steadily that Filo and Yang approached a venture capital firm to look for funding.

Ironically, it was the very success of companies such as eBay and Yahoo! that had succeeded through deliberative action that became the proof points alluded to by those who would argue for "turning on a dime." McGraw notes, "If you don't understand the transition from opportunity to execution, you end up with lots of fits and starts. The worst feeling in the world is making a decision and you're guessing—you have 10% fact."

Always Have Alternatives

"Pick a strategy and go with it." "Don't look back and don't get distracted." "Don't switch horses in the middle of the stream." But what if the strategy isn't working?

Strategy as a concept is steeped in war. It refers to planning based on knowledge of the battle terrain, comparative armed strength, and anticipating and countering one's enemy's moves. War is a good metaphor for strategy even in business terms. No battle commander would consider a battle plan that didn't have a

> **No battle commander would consider a battle plan that didn't have a contingency plan. Alternative actions are always part of the whole.**

contingency plan. Alternative actions are always part of the whole.

In 1993, when Lou Gerstner was picked to replace John Akers at the helm of IBM, the company had lost $4.97 billion, let go more than 117,000 employees, and written off more than $28 billion in restructuring charges. To the outgoing CEO and the board that had named him and was now replacing him, the solution was to break up the company into smaller, independent parts. And Gerstner was chosen, most assumed, to effect that dismemberment.

To his credit, though, Gerstner was not convinced this was the best solution. No one could accuse him of acting reflexively. After starting his new job on April 1, 1993, Gerstner spent over half his time traveling and visiting company sites. He also brought in the top 12 IBM managers and asked them to provide him with a "concise, honest appraisal of their busi-nesses." He wanted no more than a five-page report that answered these five questions:

❑ What business are you in?
❑ Who are your customers?
❑ What's your marketplace?
❑ What are your strengths and weaknesses?
❑ Who are your main competitors?

Twenty-six days later, at his first annual IBM shareholders meeting, Gerstner disclosed four objectives he had set for himself:

❑ Paring IBM to a more efficient size,
❑ Developing a strategy that would make clear which businesses the company would focus on,
❑ Decentralizing decision making, and
❑ Taking more care with IBM's customers.

Nowhere in his talk did he address the issue of dismem-berment. Yet, he was being urged strongly by shareholders, analysts, and media to move ahead with those plans. One shareholder said, "There are two or three $10 billion or $12 billion companies slopping around in there that don't neces-sarily have to be under one tent." To which Gerstner replied that he saw little sense in "tossing a fragmentation grenade" into IBM to "atomize" it.

Around this time, Gerstner chose Jerome B. York as his chief financial officer. York, who had held that job at Chrysler Corporation, had a reputation as a no-nonsense, operations-savvy CFO. He would ultimately be the one who asked the difficult questions and made sure the downsizing was handled without equivocation.

We all know that Gerstner decided not to disassemble IBM, but that was an alternative strategy that few, if any, were recommending at that time. He could have let the chips fall where they may and implemented Aker's and the board's plan to break up Big Blue. But he kept an open mind that allowed for a different solution.

The problem, Gerstner discovered, wasn't corporate bureaucracy creating inefficiencies in otherwise streamlined business units. The problem was inefficiencies within the units themselves. All that a breakup would have accomplished would have been to replace one inefficient entity with several smaller, inefficient entities. Rather, as Gerstner clearly saw, the solution lay in reengineering so that the inefficient business units became more efficient.

LOOKING FORWARD

Recessions end. Recoveries begin. "But," as McGraw asked rhetorically, "the question we need to continually pose is what will we recover to?" Since the past is no predictor of future prospects, businesses need to carefully assess realistic growth rates. It is easy, and rather common, for management to simply set aggressive double-digit growth targets to "motivate the troops." But

> **It is easy, and rather common, for management to simply set aggressive double-digit growth targets to "motivate the troops."**

when the prevailing global economic climate is one of slow or sluggish growth, what reasonable chance do most companies have of being the lone hyper-growth exception?

Continually setting overly ambitious growth targets actually saps motivation and ultimately causes management's credibility to weaken. While most businesses understand the need to monitor sector and competitor conditions, not every company attunes itself to the larger macro-economic environment, particularly when it comes to productivity. From 1995 through 2000, average productivity gains were higher than ever. But how much was due to the expansion and is, therefore, cyclical? And how much is structural and is, therefore, sustainable? The answer is more than just an interesting academic discussion. Rather, as McGraw states, "it can help us determine our speed limit." In so doing, it also helps us to establish more thoughtful growth rates.

There is a relationship between productivity growth and enhanced living standards. During the two decades of low productivity growth (e.g., 1.5%) from 1972 through 1992, most of us witnessed the attrition in living standards firsthand. By the same token, we've all enjoyed the benefits of the five years of higher productivity rates. During the last five years (1995–2000), we measured an average 3.0% productivity growth, with a peak productivity growth of 5.0% in 2000.

New evidence suggests that the gain in productivity from 3.0 to a peak of 5.0 was driven by both economic expansion and a huge increase in information technology investment. Such investment increases "capital deepening" (the capital employed per worker), which, in turn, increases productivity. Thus the level of IT investment ties to productivity upticks. It therefore stands to reason that those companies that aggressively trim their R&D and technology spending during a downturn may find themselves at a slight productivity disadvantage compared with competitors that do not.

Leading executives try to raise the sights of their team, challenge them to reach tough goals and be disciplined in all stages of the sales process. But these leaders understand that momentum is best maintained when growth, sales, and productivity targets reflect a thoughtful consideration of the full range of market conditions. It is well to look at internal productivity prospects and limitations and it is advisable to assess the health and robustness of one's industry base. But it is equally important not to overlook the global economic environment in which one is competing. A market recovery does not necessarily mean a return to 20% year-on-year growth, nor does a decline mean a precipitous drop. Savvy managers do not rely on the conventional wisdom of the past. Instead, they extend the knowledge of the past by adapting it to current conditions.

CHAPTER FOUR

The Heard and the Herd

A gile businesses communicate. They communicate internally so their managers and employees are all on the same page. And they communicate externally so that customers, suppliers, investors, analysts, and other stakeholders know what they are doing and why. They believe the maxim "perception is reality" and test perceptions frequently. When the perceptions and realities diverge, they take steps to bring them back in line. The communications process is continuous regardless of the macroeconomic state. Unlike other companies (the herd) that go silent during tumultuous times, agile businesses (the heard) may even turn up the volume.

As any seasoned politician will tell you, it's best to know what your audience is already thinking before deciding what you're going to say. We'll examine some examples of perception testing and how, by using the results to frame communications objectives and messaging strategies, you can avoid corporate identity crises and market confusion. We'll also look at the need for, and benefits associated with, effective internal and external communications and how they help support corporate vision, marketing strategies, and brand management. But it all begins with a healthy dose of self-examination.

WHO ARE YOU NOW?

Who do you think you are? Who do your constituents think you are? You'd be surprised at the disparities that occur. One of the reasons for continuous communication is to ensure that your audiences are kept up to date with changes in your company.

Corporate identity is critical, but before doing anything to change or reinforce that image, it makes sense first to find out how your partners, customers, and the media perceive your company, its brand, and its products. Companies that place a premium on researching what guides their customers' buying decisions ratchet up profits through improved hit rates and more effective and targeted marketing and communications. As the example below shows, sometimes it's like taking candy from a baby.

Masterfoods USA runs four of the ten highest volume candy brands in the United States, brands such as M&Ms and Skittles. The company certainly understands what it means to keep its product line fresh and interesting, particularly when its prime demographic consists of impetuous youth. The company has succeeded, breathing life into brands that in some cases are 70 years old, by leveraging the strength of core brands to launch new line extensions and by careful innovation in both product development and product marketing. When consumer research conducted by Masterfoods showed that stalwart Snickers fans occasionally yearned for a snack food that made noise, Masterfoods launched Snickers Cruncher. Sales for the new extension exceeded $100m in its first year.

One of the company's more interesting consumer experiments occurred in January 2002, with Masterfoods' lead M&M product. In what was the largest campaign in company history, *Promo Magazine* reported that Masterfoods launched a "Global Color Vote" in which people from 78 countries could vote their choice of a new M&M color. As one press release noted, "The effort in January received more media attention than most overseas elections." Masterfoods VP Ellis Rowe attributes their longstanding product and brand success to intensive consumer research. "This may be candy we're talking about," he says, "but it's not child's play, and there are piles of psychographics hiding behind impulse purchases."

> *Promo Magazine* **reported that Masterfoods launched a 'Global Color Vote' in which people from 78 countries could vote their choice of a new M&M color. As one press release noted, "The effort in January received more media attention than most overseas elections.**

Mergers and acquisitions can also confuse the external perception of a company's identity and brand. Citibank faced this particular challenge a few years ago when it merged with Travelers Group to form Citigroup. Sandy Weill, the company's CEO, required his management team to perform exhaustive research to understand where there was consonance or dissonance in the market's perception of the company's core products.

The research determined that there was a fair amount of overlap in credit cards, consumer lending, asset management, and private banking. To resolve this problem, according to strategy consultant Andrew Pierce, Citigroup resorted to establishing "clear boundaries among brands targeted to distinct consumer segments with unique value propositions." Companies that are less studied in their approach tend to view their products or services as a "disparate collection of individual brands," says Pierce. But by doing so, they blur the perceived value of individual products, offering customers a jumbled brand portfolio instead of a strongly differentiated line.

Unless you first decide what image you want to convey and survey your constituents to see what perception they already have, you cannot know how best to proceed. You can end up spending a lot more than you need on image transformation or not spending enough.

INTERNAL COMMUNICATIONS

Many companies pay a lot more attention to external communications than internal communications. Agile businesses do not make that mistake. It is just as important to inform your own people as it is to talk to customers, investors, media, and analysts. Most of our CEO interviewees agreed their people can handle the truth no matter where it leads; what they can't handle is lack of information.

In "Lessons in Authentic Leadership," Daniel Elash and James Long talk about the flip side to communications—the ability to be a good listener. "If you want to lead, you'd better know how to listen to what is going on in your organization. ... If you are going to inspire, mentor, stretch and retain today's workers, you have to hear what they are saying. ... A leader has to create the listening posts in order to ensure that forums for peer-to-peer conversations and the 'third places' for dialogues about the work exist across both internal and external boundaries."

In general, CEOs who have established a reputation for timely, open, and honest internal communications have found that morale has remained strong even under the most trying circumstances. And when an executive team starts out with executive pay cuts before instituting broader pay cuts, it demonstrates to the employees that the leaders are taking responsibility for the problems and are trying to confine the remedies to those in control.

A well-developed and executed internal communications program can alleviate workplace anxiety. It will also help align what's being said externally with what's being said internally, particularly during times of change. Technology can help to enhance the internal communications process. Hewlett-Packard, for example, makes excellent use of its worldwide, closed-circuit television network to communicate with all its facilities and employees. A well-organized and timed use of internal communications helps promote employee confidence and can be used to turn those employees into a worldwide team of brand ambassadors.

Adds Jim Morgan, "You have a lot fewer problems if you make sure the bad news is out. Downturns used to trickle in gradually over a couple of quarters. But now everyone has the same information and that leads to abrupt ups and downs." You don't want this to happen with your employees. You want to manage consistency and keep productivity up. After every quarterly earnings report, Morgan dispatches his managers to meet with every employee across the world. Employees are given an explanation for why the earnings are up or down and what the projections and outlook are. Doing so is a sign of respect and employees like to feel respected.

Said Adrian Slywotzky, Mercer Management Consulting vice president, "Companies must intensify marketing and communications—recession or no recession. You always need a message to galvanize your people around. In a recession, you have the undivided attention of every person in your organization. That's why it may be the easiest time to change habits."

> **"In a recession, you have the undivided attention of every person in your organization. That's why it may be the easiest time to change habits."**
> **—Adrian Slywotzky, Vice President, Mercer Management Consulting**

As you'll read in chapter five, internal communications has an important part to play in all aspects of a performance culture. It is an essential tool for achieving consensus on key strategies and objectives and an ongoing means for keeping people's actions aligned with those strategies and objectives.

EXTERNAL COMMUNICATIONS

What do your constituents know and how does that affect their expectations? The answer is crucial because it will influence your relationships with customers, suppliers, distributors, market analysts, and the media. There's no way to overstate the importance of psychology in investment trends, but it's also a vitally important factor in business behavior. It affects the risks we're willing to take and how long we're willing to wait for returns on investments. By conditioning a market for what to expect and when to expect it, we're establishing the range of expectations rather than leaving it to chance. Therefore, three important objectives for external communications are:

> **By conditioning a market for what to expect and when to expect it, we're establishing the range of expectations rather than leaving it to chance.**

❑ Managing external perceptions,

❑ Conditioning the market, and

❑ Describing the big picture.

Managing External Perceptions

Agile leaders make it a point to frequently communicate with the media and take part in panel discussions. Rather than announcing new initiatives in a vacuum, they see their role as one of creating a context. To that end, their communications strategy aims at four objectives:

❑ Describing the opportunities,

❑ Describing the capabilities needed and possessed,

❑ Setting the market stage, and
❑ Establishing credibility.

These leaders focus on setting context for their communications.

For example, in describing the opportunity to serve the Mexican market with educational books, McGraw doesn't talk about textbooks, he talks about numbers—the numbers of students who attend school in compulsory grades one through six, the smaller numbers that continue past grade six, and the even smaller numbers that go on to college. He talks about McGraw-Hill's facilities and talent in Mexico and political initiatives to raise the country's educational standards. He also discusses financials and profitability, painting a cogent, credible picture of an opportunity his company has the capabilities, experience, and connections to pursue. McGraw also deliberately puts himself before the press at least once a quarter to set the stage for his results. He doesn't want McGraw-Hill to be lumped with all publishing houses in the mind of his constituents. He wants to educate the market about precisely what McGraw-Hill is, does, and is setting out to do.

McGraw's communications efforts are cumulative. He has established relationships with the media he feels are most appropriate, and each visit is more of an ongoing saga than a restatement of basic talking points. "You begin the saga with the basic 'who are we,' and that becomes the foundation upon which the rest is ultimately built," he explained.

COMMUNICATIONS AS TRUST BUILDER

At the root of every business transaction and relationship is trust, and there's no better time to build or reinforce trust than during an economic contraction. As we discussed in *Security Transformation*, trust is perhaps the most important factor in trade. If you and your company are trusted to share the good news and the bad, there's a direct relationship between that trust and the confidence, loyalty, and retention of your constituents—investors, customers, and employees.

Every CEO would love a chance to talk about a major market success or a glowing quarterly result. No one wants the spotlight on him or her after taking a huge write-off or reporting a large, unexpected loss. But that's also the CEO's job. Going quiet can worsen speculation and erode confidence, both inside and outside the organization.

Applied's Morgan said it best: "No news is bad news, bad news is good news, and good news is no news." As we wrote earlier, everyone chafes at a lack of information, so no news is bad news. In fact, in the absence of information, people tend to fill in the blanks, and those inserts are often far worse than what's really going on. Bad news is good news because, as Morgan pointed out, "when times are tough, you want to hear the worst as quickly as possible so that you can be aware, prepared, and take action." Morgan sees good news as no news because it tells you what you already know, for example, that you're on track. But while it may not be news, good news is important because the additional message is that the strategy is sound, management is handling things competently, and the company is in good shape.

Unless the economic cycle should cease, bad news is inevitable. And sometimes even unpredictable things happen. When they do, though, how you and your company handle them is very telling, and trust is very much at stake. Two classic examples of diametrically opposite tactics and results help to cement this point.

The Right Thing

In 1982, it was discovered that Tylenol capsules in ostensibly unopened bottles had been tampered with and poisoned. At the time, Tylenol capsules were Johnson & Johnson's biggest-selling products. James Burke, then chairman, was unequivocal about the response. He wanted an immediate recall of all Tylenol capsules. He insisted that the company keep the media and the public fully briefed on all aspects of its internal investigation as to source and method of tampering. In short, Burke made sure that Johnson & Johnson demonstrated its priority of public welfare over corporate profits. Tylenol's market share dropped to 18%, but within a year of the first tampering incident, it rebounded to 28%.

The Wrong Thing

Shortly after midnight on December 3, 1984, a Union Carbide pesticide plant in Bhopal, India, accidentally released approximately 40 metric tons of the chemical methyl isocyanate into the atmosphere. The incident resulted in an estimated 2000 casualties, 100,000 injuries, and significant damage to livestock and crops. Union Carbide's tactics, in the aftermath, were right out of the movie *The China Syndrome*. The company was evasive. Officials were defensive. It looked like a company under siege. Fingers were pointing in all directions and no one knew anything. Of course, the incident raised questions about chemical-plant safety, but Union Carbide's response may well have damaged its reputation and diminished its brand "equity."

Clearly, these are two extremes. A disappointing quarter is nothing compared with poisoned pain relievers and toxic chemical leaks. But they show that, even in the short term and certainly over the long term, the better tactic is open communication. Obfuscation and equivocation will be perceived as evasiveness. Evasion, in turn, begets fear. Fearful employees look for other jobs. Fearful customers look for other sources. And fearful investors look for other stocks.

THE HERD REACTS

During the peak of the economic expansion, companies were paying PR agencies millions of dollars to look for opportunities to express themselves. Everyone had something to say, and new magazines and periodicals couldn't be turned out fast enough to accommodate them all. The noise level was deafening at times and it seemed as if, no matter how much money one spent on PR and advertising, it just wasn't enough.

In the economic contraction that followed, many of the newest publications were either on the ropes or were down for the count. Advertising page count dwindled. And, yet even with fewer editorial pages to fill, magazines and newspapers were having trouble filling them because of companies that were reticent to talk. Businesses pared their PR and advertising budgets to the bone, and PR agencies and advertising firms cut back staff to subsistence levels.

Their (the herd's) corporate thinking is evident, but the rationale is wrong. "If I don't have something positive to say, I shouldn't say anything at all," executives reason. The rationale is that only good news is persuasive. Bad news will cause the market to lose confidence. But this notion is wrongheaded. What the silence does is prolong indecision about buying, about employment, about investment. We know less about what companies are thinking now than we did two years ago. We're not sure what they are seeing or what opportunities they are pursuing. We read about billions in venture capital poised for investment but currently "parked." We continue to witness the seesawing of share prices with strings of back-to-back gains limited to four days or less. Some companies announce growth in new orders, but the momentum is tepid. With no news on which to anchor decisions, people simply wait—and wait.

We know less about what companies are thinking now than we did two years ago.

The root of every economic turnaround is a resurgence in optimism, both business and consumer. That resurgence of confidence will not happen in an environment of guarded news. It needs context, logic, and a sense that the gears are turning again. This last recession was atypical. Consumer spending remained relatively strong throughout. It was business-to-business commerce that took the hit, particularly in the technology sector. It's important to remember there was real growth in this economy before the emergence of the dot.com bubble. Communications will help remind us that there is real growth potential in the wake of the dot.com demise.

COMMUNICATING FOR STRATEGIC ADVANTAGE

At any time, a CEO can use communications for strategic advantage. At times when other CEOs are keeping a low profile, opportunities often abound. Business and market strategies typically all have their communications components. The examples that follow simply show how a communications strategy, coupled with communications tactics, can make a significant difference in ultimate market outcome.

Changing the Terms of the Market Battle

Back in 1980, Intel was locked in a protracted competitive battle over design wins for its 16-bit microprocessors. The PC market was still embryonic and no major product category held sway. One of Intel's competitors had a definite advantage with its leading microprocessor. It had far greater appeal to software engineers who were then emerging as the key design-in decision makers. Intel's primary advantage was that it offered a much richer assortment of companion chips for its microprocessors. At the time, though, the battle was being fought at the product level and Intel's competitor had the upper hand.

Intel, realizing it couldn't win on the basis of a microprocessor-to-microprocessor comparison, decided to wage a multifaceted battle focused on both a top-down and bottom-up campaign. The first salvo was a major story in *Business Week* with the company's founders, Gordon Moore and Robert Noyce, looking over a huge chessboard. The accompanying top-down story was about vision and complete solutions. The two leaders showed how their divisions and product offerings were all driven by a unified view of how best to support their original equipment manufacturer (OEM) customers. Without talking about their microprocessors, memories, co-processors, or intelligent controllers, the pair included all the business units and their products in the big picture they painted. In doing so, they elevated the discussion from a microprocessor-to-microprocessor comparison to a solutions-delivery comparison. On that score, Intel had the advantage.

Within months of that *Business Week* story, the tide began to change. Intel's divisions were announcing new products, and each launch was tied back to the big-picture story context. They achieved the right balance of corporate and business unit communications. In addition to new-product announcements, Intel was busy submitting authored articles to trade magazines showing how complete systems could be built using various combinations of its integrated circuits (ICs). Upper-level managers were becoming persuaded that Intel had a better overall solution strategy. In 1981, IBM launched its PC and Intel's microprocessor was in it. That launch set the stage for the full gestation of the PC market and, with it, a rapid ramp-up in unit volume and microprocessor volume.

Before the original confrontation came to a head, Intel's top two leaders had left the communications objectives up to the business units. The result was a largely business unit view of things. The memory unit pushed its memory products, the microcontroller unit marketed its chips, and the microprocessor group did its own thing. It wasn't until top management elected to own the communications objectives that a credible, overarching strategy was described in which all the business units and their products fit so nicely.

> It wasn't until top management elected to own the communications objectives that a credible, overarching strategy was described in which all the business units and their products fit so nicely.

The Intel example shows that by creating a balanced communications effort, agile businesses are able to create a big-picture view of their companies and markets. The big picture serves as a foundation for prior as well as subsequent product and service announcements. And with each new complementary introduction, the company's ability to visualize and execute gains more credibility. If it does it well, a company can achieve strong symbiosis.

Changing the Market's Purchase-Decision Criteria

The preceding example was about computer chips; this one is about another kind of chip. First invented in the 1850s in the United States, potato chips are lucrative products to be sure. Try to imagine any kind of party without chips and dip. According to a story in *The Christian Science Monitor* (October 23, 2001), Frito-Lay's factories produce 13 million bags of potato chips daily, or 3.9 trillion bags per year.

Incumbent potato-chip competitors were chagrined when Procter & Gamble introduced its Pringles product to the market. Unlike the other chips, thinly sliced potatoes that are fried then salted, Pringles were made using a mash produced from potato flakes. Instead of a potpourri of sizes and shapes, each Pringles "chip" was exactly the same size and shape. What's more, Pringles were further differentiated by being packed and sold in a cylindrical container instead of the familiar bag. The product took the market by storm, and its growth in revenues came primarily as a result of usurpation of market share.

According to Al Ries and Jack Trout, in their book *Positioning: The Battle for Your Mind*, potato-chip competitors were having little success in turning back the onslaught simply by increasing the frequency of their advertising and loss-leading promotions. But someone came up with a great idea. They focused on the differences between the ingredients labels of Pringles and those of mainstream potato chips. Pringles had a lot of unpronounceable ingredients. The others had potatoes, oil, and salt, primarily. By making these differences the issue, rather than the novel shape and container, potato-chip makers were able to blunt the assault upon their revenues and profits. In essence, by using communications to point out some undesirable differences, Pringles' competitors were able to inject new factors into consumer purchase-decision criteria.

REINFORCING YOUR BRAND

Agile business CEOs make brand reinforcement a priority. They make sure that cost management does not compromise brand management. And they do their part, through communications, in giving context to the various products or services their companies provide.

As for the debate over whether product or brand is the more compelling sales success factor, we believe unequivocally that both play critical roles and are extremely interdependent. When it comes to this debate, conversation can become heated. During the World Economic Forum in New York City in early 2002, one panelist insisted that brand mattered for little. It was the quality of the product, at the end of the day, that mattered. Another panelist flatly refuted this, stating that a strong product rides on the coattails of a strong brand. In short order, both panelists became quite animated and left their seats to make their points standing.

In short order, both panelists became quite animated and left their seats to make their points standing. No question, the brand/product controversy is an emotive discussion.

No question, the brand/product controversy is an emotive discussion. In our view, though, neither one is preeminent. Brand and product work symbiotically. A strong brand brings many positive associative traits to a product and can help a new product break through the clutter and attract the attention of a prospective buyer. If you love Pepsi, chances are you might be willing to gamble on the brand in an unproven category. Likewise, good products speak for themselves. They act to either burnish or tarnish a brand accordingly. Product brands themselves have lifted some otherwise unknown companies to great heights.

Branding is not a slogan, nor a logo. Neither is it a mission statement. Branding is a culmination of all the large and small things companies do to make their customers' experience distinctive. It is a dynamic notion in customers' minds—not on product shelves—that morphs with the changes in customer choices and distribution channels. Branding is not something you do once, then leave on automatic pilot. It is no guarantee that customers will be loyal to you and your products when compelling alternatives are available. Branding is more qualitative than quantitative, more intangible than tangible.

Branding is not a slogan, nor a logo. Neither is it a mission statement. Branding is a culmination of all the large and small things companies do to make their customers' experience distinctive.

During any economic phase, branding is important. It raises the stakes above pure price competition. It elevates the discussion above a point-by-point comparison of features. It is where some of the more qualitative differences weigh in, such as after-sale service, pride of ownership, and sense of style. Branding is especially important where companies grow through mergers and acquisitions. The merging of two companies with equally strong brands can be a problem, if the intent is to emerge with one very strong brand.

"We've gained control of or acquired some national companies, and there is brand legacy to deal with," said Chris Gent, Vodafone's chief executive. "First we co-brand, then move toward exclusive branding. Our goal is for the Vodafone brand to ascend." Two national companies that

Vodafone acquired were a German and an Italian, both having very strong brands. Vodafone chose to reinforce its brand by having a German driving a striking red Ferrari. The champion driver was Michael Schumacher, the champion car was a Formula One Ferrari, and red is the color of Vodafone's brand. "Over 360 million viewers per fortnight see this commercial," Gent explained, "and it's our subtle way of blending the two strong brands into the ultimate Vodafone brand."

There are differences of opinion over when and whether to reinforce corporate or product brands. Some companies will defer to the product. Diageo is a great example. Have you heard of Diageo? It's more than likely you've heard of its brands, such premier names as Johnnie Walker, Guinness, Smirnoff, J&B, Baileys, Cuervo, Tanqueray, and Captain Morgan. Likewise, some readers may be unfamiliar with corporate giant, Reed Elsevier, but may be well acquainted with its diverse holdings, including LexisNexis, Martindale-Hubbell, Harcourt Publishing, and Holt, Rinehart and Winston.

In an economic contraction, consumers and purchasing agents usually have less to spend and take more time making purchase decisions. Whereas sales of a particular category of product may fall, they typically don't fall proportionately for every make. The difference is often one of branding.

If a company has done a good job of managing its brand, which entails consistent product quality, responsive customer service, consistent messaging, and the like, then it is probably benefiting from it by less revenue attrition. If you compare the proportionate loss of sales among companies in a particular market segment, those with the strongest brands typically suffer less. Therefore, an economic contraction is not the time to undermine your branding efforts by indiscriminate cost reductions. While others may be compromising their brand strengths, you can bolster yours just by continuing to manage it well. While the contraction continues, you'll benefit from fewer lost sales, and once the recovery begins, your well-managed brand will provide additional competitive advantage.

According to work done by McGraw-Hill Research involving relative performance analysis of 600 industrial companies, those that maintained or increased their advertising expenditures in the 1981/1982 recession averaged significantly higher sales growth both during and after the recession. By 1985, for example, these companies enjoyed an average sales growth of 275% over the preceding five years. In contrast, those that reduced their investment in advertising advanced only 19% over the same period.

BE HEARD

When a CEO describes a strategy, a product, or a service as "one of the best kept secrets" in a market, there's something wrong. They didn't try to keep it secret; they failed to get it any attention. Agile business CEOs understand and use the power of communications. They use it to refine strategies and keep performance teams in alignment. They use it to set and manage stakeholder expectations. They see communications as a key element of corporate and market strategies and use it to their advantage. Communications is an important part of building and preserving trust. And it's a major component of brand reinforcement and management. Like cost management and organizational efficiency, communications needs to be a fundamental and continuous business discipline. Communications is built in and always "on," regardless of economic conditions.

CHAPTER FIVE

New Strategies for an Uncertain World

"**S**trategy and tactics." All business and marketing plans are punctuated with these terms for which we have the Greeks to thank. Strategy in the time of ancient Greece was not used in the context of business; it was always used in the context of war. Strategy was, and still is, a way to gain advantage by anticipating what your adversary (or competitor) is likely to do when confronted with a variety of challenges.

It works best when the variables are both identifiable and few and when certainty of likely responses is high. It can fail, miserably, when options change but strategies remain fixed. After World War I, France had built its "Maginot Line" using a strategy based on the certainties of trench warfare, but the options for Germany had changed (through use of airplanes and tanks), and that strategy failed to protect France.

For decades after World War II, the pace of change and innovation in industry was such that companies could adopt Maginot-Line-like strategies and succeed. But today's markets have their own forms of "blitzkrieg" options and strategies cast in concrete are an anachronism.

STRATEGIES AND OBJECTIVES

Successful business begins with strategies and objectives. These strategies have to be consistent with the structure of an industry and levels of uncertainty. The manifestation of a strategy is a posture coupled with appropriate actions.

Business agility includes the strategic flexibility needed to thrive when market infrastructures are being broken down and reconstructed and the organizational flexibility that avoids mismatches between changing approaches and current business models. Traditional business strategic planning and execution grew in an environment where industries had stable infrastructures and innovations evolved relatively slowly. Strategy was defined "as an integrated set of actions leading to a sustainable

> **Business agility includes the strategic flexibility needed to thrive when market infrastructures are being broken down and the organizational flexibility that avoids mismatches between changing approaches and current business models.**

competitive advantage," according to McKinsey & Co. Today, with few exceptions, this definition no longer applies. Markets evolve at a much higher rate of speed and innovations abound, creating varying levels of uncertainty.

Changes in markets and business can have profound

effects upon strategies. For example, as information technology has grown more standards-based and multi-vendor in nature, companies often have to be willing to sacrifice one division's interest in favor of a bigger deal. Before the big push for standards and multi-vendor compatibilities, the larger IT companies were used to providing the whole solution—systems, service, and maintenance. They had to learn new skills, though, once their customers began specifying multi-vendor systems.

One vendor had to take responsibility (called the "prime") and make sure all vendor products and services performed as expected. Suddenly a company such as HP, as a prime vendor, might have to take responsibility for IBM and/or Sun Microsystems hardware in addition to its own. In other cases, a third-party integrator took responsibility for the whole project. As multi-vendor solutions abounded, whole-solution vendors had to learn to be satisfied with a piece of the pie while keeping all their divisions adequately motivated. This has been no easy task.

TRADITIONAL STRATEGIC APPROACH

The traditional strategic approach looked at industries according to Porter's model. In it, the industry was seen as consisting of a set of unrelated buyers, suppliers, substitutes, and competitors, all interacting at arm's length. The industry's competitors were affected by endogenous forces (e.g., those that are part of the industry), such as suppliers, new entrants, buyers, and substitutes, and exogenous forces (e.g., those that are external to the industry but influence it), such as macroeconomics, technology, regulation, and customer preferences.

Furthermore, competitive advantage (and value) went to those companies able to erect effective barriers to competition. In other words, competitive advantage was structural. And, finally, uncertainty in these industries was low enough to enable making accurate predictions about competitive behavior.

The idea that an industry is rational and that each competitor operates at arm's length with the others no longer represents most industries. In addition to arm's-length relationships, we also have cross-industry structures that include alliances, networks, and economic webs, and relationships where firms are singled out for favored treatment based on financial interest and other factors (e.g., Japan's *keiretsus* and Korea's *chaebols*). In many industries, the relationships are anything but arm's length.

We also need to look at the idea that competitive advantage is primarily structural. In fact, in some industries companies outperform competitors with great execution rather than structural barriers, such as patented processes or advanced technologies. In addition, other companies compete successfully and create wealth through intellectual property. Rambus and ARM Semiconductor, for example, earn most of their revenues through licensing intellectual property (IP). Thus, structural differences no longer account for all differences in competitive advantage. Execution and IP often count more.

INCREASED LEVELS OF UNCERTAINTY

The idea that industries exist in an environment of low uncertainty is now obsolete. The pace of innovation has changed that notion forever. Industries that seem to exist in an environment of low uncertainty today can become highly uncertain tomorrow. Just consider the effect of deregulation on airlines, electric power utilities, and telecommunications. Consider the abrupt changes in package delivery services once FedEx proved that overnight delivery was possible, affordable, and profitable.

The ability to send digital information over analog phone lines was the impetus for the telephone modem industry. Bandwidth limits were predictable—about 30,000 bits per second—and the telecom industry began preparing a new service, Integrated Services Digital Network (ISDN), which would permit bandwidths of over 100,000 bits per second. But then we learned we could raise the dialup modem rate to 56,000 bits per second, and the cable operators figured out how to offer much higher download speeds using cable channels and cable modems. In response, the phone companies figured out how to match that bandwidth using existing copper telephone wiring (e.g., DSL), and the race was on.

We know that strategies have to account for uncertainty. A modem maker may have opted to tool up to make ISDN modems before the advent of cable modems and DSL, and that strategy would have seemed sound. After the advent of the two broadband technologies, that ISDN strategy would have been shaky. If the ISDN strategy allowed for no flexibility, it could have been fatal.

Yogi Berra, the erstwhile Yankee catcher, said, "The future ain't what it used to be." Well, neither is strategy. Varying levels of uncertainty force us to adopt strategies with varying levels of equivocation. Some companies enter an industry with a strategy bent on changing or *transforming* its status quo; others adopt strategies meant to *adapt* to that status quo but differentiate through better marketing or execution.

> Some companies enter an industry with a strategy bent on changing or transforming its status quo; others adopt strategies meant to adapt to that status quo but differentiate through better marketing or execution.

As an example of a transforming strategy, Amazon.com clearly entered the book business intending to shake it up, and it did. Webvan hoped to do the same in the grocery business, but failed. The upside potential of an industry transformation strategy can be quite high, and the downside potential, devastating.

Microsoft's Xbox entry in the video games console business appears to be an adaptor strategy. From a pricing and distribution standpoint, it is hard to distinguish Xbox from Sony's or Nintendo's consoles. Microsoft is not making consumers choose a new way to interface games and televisions. Nor is it trying to create a novel way for players to control their games. It has taken a far less risky approach to this market than a transformation strategy, and while the upside potential may be more muted, so is the downside risk.

A third general strategy is an equivocal-intent-to-participate one. Here, a company reserves its right to play—maybe. Random Ventures' Xlibris adopted this strategy with e-books. The publisher of paper and e-books codeveloped with Adobe a means of securely distributing e-books over the Internet. But Richard Sarnoff, president of Random House New Media and Corporate Development, considers the effort somewhat embryonic. No one knows, yet, what device readers will choose for reading e-books. Until that becomes more certain, Xlibris has given itself permission to take part without having had to invest huge amounts of money on uncertain infrastructure. By adopting this strategy, Xlibris can invest in organizational capability and study various approaches and formats without making big-bet investments in what is still a highly uncertain market.

Transformer, adaptor, or equivocal-intent-to-participate, the strategy one chooses should reflect the level of uncertainty in an industry and the risk one is willing to accept. Agile businesses seem to know when to transform and when to adapt. And adapting seems to be the strategy of choice in most cases.

In the *Financial Times*, in October 2001, a feature headlined "Lessons from the dot.com days" said, "Businesses that avoid expending resources on trials of strength (such as Netscape squaring off with Microsoft) are more likely to succeed. In contrast with failed giant-killers, such as Netscape, the new economy's successes have prospered by minimizing the threat of head-to-head conflict. In addition, these companies have learned to compete in ways that prevent competitors from taking full advantage of their strengths." Here, eBay's strategy of collaborating with rather than challenging AOL is a good example. Both companies benefit from the arrangement, and AOL has less incentive to challenge eBay with its own auction service.

LOOKING FORWARD, REASONING BACKWARD

Referring to the then-upcoming FCC spectrum auctions, *The Economist* wrote in 1994, "As for the firms that want to get their hands on a sliver of the airwaves, their best bet is to go out first and hire themselves a good game theorist."

"Game Theory, long an intellectual pastime, came into its own as a business tool," said *Forbes* in July 1995. "Game theory is hot," wrote *The Wall Street Journal* in February 1995.

All of these stories referred to an old theory being applied to new strategies. As mentioned earlier, strategy is based on anticipating your adversary's response to a variety of challenges. Game theory provides a systematic approach for analyzing the rational (and, therefore, likely) responses to a variety of moves.

Tom Copeland, chief corporate finance officer and head of Monitor Corporate Finance, said, "Game theory can explain why oligopolies tend to be unprofitable, the cycle of over-capacity and overbuilding, and the tendency to execute real options earlier than optimal."

Game theory as applied to business strategy begins with the assumption that one is self-interested and selfish, and so is everyone else. According to McKinsey & Co., "A good game theorist gets inside the heads of other players to understand their economic incentives and likely behavior."

Game theory examines the players, their strategies, and the payoffs to each that result from their collective actions and responses. In a perfect world, if everyone's objectives are accurately depicted and everyone's actions are rational, then the total number of possibilities can be whittled down to those that make the most sense for each player. The result will be fewer likely moves and countermoves and a much higher degree of predictability. That's the theory, anyway.

If all airline companies, for example, were to apply game theory, then a situation where one precipitates a protracted "lose-lose" fare war would be highly unlikely. But we've seen our share of those. Similarly, if the semiconductor manufacturers had all used game theory, then fewer of them would have invested in mega-fabrication facilities, thus creating the conditions for oversupply and commensurate price softening. Well-executed game theory might also have mitigated the current slump in the telecom industry by showing the effect of all the players pursuing increased capacity at the same time.

It does this by including the timing of moves in the calculation. Simultaneous actions or moves, for example, produce very different results than sequential ones. In addition, game theory looks at moves and payoffs where players compete or cooperate. Such an exercise, for example, might have validated the wisdom of eBay's cooperating with rather than competing with AOL.

As with many systematic approaches to business and marketing strategy, though, there is the risk of:

❑ Over-reliance on the analysis results,
❑ Oversimplifications,
❑ Assumption of rational behavior, and
❑ Failure to properly discern other players' objectives.

One difference between business strategy and chess is that chess has immutable rules whereas business competition essentially has none. As a result, move and countermove analysis in business is always imperfect, making analysis results imperfect. With multiple players and multiple strategies, the analysis matrix can become quite untenable. Simplification becomes mandatory, but probabilities of oversimplification increase.

Rational behavior is influenced by the data one has at hand and the interpretation of that data. Game theory assumes all the players have common knowledge, but in reality, in business, not all the players will have the same data, nor will they all interpret it in like manner.

And game theory depends heavily upon the correct objectives being ascribed to each player. Assuming all players will act in ways that optimize profitability will lead to erroneous analysis for those players whose objectives are focused on increased market share. As such, the move/countermove analysis will be flawed, as will the payoff assumptions.

Game theory, then, is not a panacea. On the other hand, if viewed as an additional tool for making logical and informed decisions, game theory has its place.

OODA LOOPS: LESSONS OF WAR STRATEGY

OODA is the acronym for *observe, orient, decide,* and *act*. Since the concept of strategy comes to us from Greek warriors, what could be more natural than for modern business to adopt this centuries-old warrior strategy? In war, repeated OODA sequences (or loops) are aimed at getting the enemy to be where you want it to be, doing what you want it to do.

One uses OODA loops to engage one's customers— observing, orienting, deciding, and acting to move them to your products and services. It is the epitome of market shaping.

In a study by the U.S. Air Force, fighter pilots who consistently won dogfights intuitively used OODA loop strategies, sizing up an enemy's actions and preempting his move, thus confusing the opponent and capturing the initiative.

But where do OODA loops figure in the battle for the hearts, minds, and dollars of customers? Does one observe, orient, decide, and act against one's competitors, as in war? No. One uses OODA loops to engage one's customers— observing, orienting, deciding, and acting to move them to your products and services. It is the epitome of market shaping.

Here's how Mark F. Blaxill and Thomas M. Hout of the Boston Consulting Group described OODA loops applied to business strategy:

> Fast-response companies manage their OODA loops, starting with timely observation and orientation. For example, they collect today's sales data at the retail level because wholesale data are too late and distorted. They visit advanced university labs as research is taking shape and do not just read the papers. They study their customers thoroughly from several different points of view. Reactive companies suffer late recognition and disparate views, then incur the extra cost of studies and dispute resolution to fix them.
>
> Fast-response companies accelerate decisions by better preparing the participants. They move senior executives around temporarily, forming new teams to vary the interaction patterns and fracture old assumptions. They move decisions down the corporate ladder and make the small decisions continually, without putting them off. No organizational habit is more insidious than constant formal, upward review and the need to wait for the big decision.

According to Dr. Chester Richards, a retired colonel in the Air Force Reserve with a Ph.D. in mathematics, "that innovation is related to market shaping goes back to the military idea of initiative." He notes:

> Companies take the initiative in the marketplace by offering a stream of new products and services. Where

do new products and services come from? The only answer possible, discounting elves and gamma rays, is through the initiative of the people who work for and with the organization. A market creator uses the almost symbiotic relationship all of its people have with its customers to generate ideas for new features or capabilities or whatever. [George] Stalk and [Thomas] Hout were dead on, when in the middle of describing how agile companies become entwined with their customers, they observed, "Sometimes it's difficult to know who's leading whom." (Stalk and Hout, p. 264)

Incidentally, this is the same principle underlying maneuver warfare, where an army puts out tens or hundreds of small "feelers," then uses its fast OODA loop speed to identify and reinforce those that begin to penetrate. This remarkably successful concept has been used to great effect by such leaders as Erwin Rommel, George S. Patton, Vo Nguyen Giap, Moshe Dyan, and Norman Schwarzkopf.

TURNING STRATEGIES INTO ACTIONS

As we said at the beginning of this chapter, successful business begins with strategy and objectives. Turning those strategies and objectives into coordinated and cohesive actions is where the rubber meets the road. Agile companies are especially adept at doing just that, and the common denominator is their performance cultures.

CHAPTER SIX

Creating a Performance Culture

Business agility has to permeate all aspects of a business. The ability to sense, recognize, and act decisively must become part of your culture and be reflected in the people you hire, the strategies you adopt, the systems that support you, and the values you espouse. Regardless of the industries they're in, agile businesses have performance cultures. They may differ in the specifics but all are very much alike in the essentials.

Every CEO we interviewed for this book said essentially the same thing: "The difference is the people." And it didn't matter which industry they were in either, manufacturing or services. Technology innovations would only take you so far, some advised. A great strategy without great execution is worthless, others opined. But they all agreed that it was ability of the people—managers and managed—that turned an opportunity into a successful result.

When we probed deeper, we found that it was really more than just the collective abilities of the people in a company that

If the right things were measured, in the right way, and the reward system was appropriately structured, then whole organizations would act in ways congruent with key corporate strategies.

made it successful. It was the ability of management to develop appropriate strategies and match them with actions. In addition, they were able to convey strategic and tactical objectives in a way that helped others align their activities to those objectives and to hire people with the skills to execute those strategies. That ability, in turn, was bolstered by clear, concise descriptions coupled with quantitative metrics and incentives. If the right things were measured, in the right way, and the reward system was appropriately structured, then whole organizations would act in ways congruent with key corporate strategies.

For example, during the last two calendar quarters of 2001, Wal-Mart quickly adopted an inventory-reduction strategy in the face of expected revenue decline. Wal-Mart challenged its "associates (employees) ... to reduce inventories by more than $1 billion," according to its CEO, H. Lee Scott. The objective was unequivocal. People were given the power to take decisive actions. Managers throughout the corporation had access to measurements associated with inventory reduction. Everyone in the company was given a variety of incentives to achieve the objective. And everyone agreed with the underlying rationale for doing so.

Implicit in the Wal-Mart example are the following:

❏ Motivated people,

❏ Consensus about strategy and objectives,

❏ Employee integration and empowerment,

❏ People who buy into the strategy and objectives,

❏ Focused execution,

❏ Relevant measurements that link operations to strategies,

❏ Reward systems that reinforce alignment of activities with objectives.

These elements constitute the core of a performance-oriented company and are the underpinnings of a performance culture. When CEOs point to people as the primary differentiator, we believe they assume these other elements are already in place and integrated. We would argue, though, that without these other elements, the talents of people could easily be misdirected and are, therefore, largely ineffective.

Changes in markets evoke changes in strategies. People need to be persuaded about the need for a change in strategy and the efficacy of any new ones. New strategies are likely to create a need for new measurements and probably the discarding of some existing ones. And, finally, reward systems may have to be altered to hasten the realignment of activities and objectives. Clearly, these elements must be flexible and adaptable. In an agile business, they are.

PRUDENT STRATEGY AND CLEAR DESCRIPTION

It is critical that everyone understand the nature of the strategy they are participating in and that the objectives complement the strategy. An adaptor strategy with unrealistically high upside expectations or a transforming strategy that downplays the downside risk can create disillusionment.

Once a key strategy has been adopted, it must be described clearly and concisely. If a consultant interviewed your company's executives and senior managers, one on one, asking about your key strategies and objectives, do you think there would be a lot of consensus? Many companies, even blue chippers, will show significant variability. This is particularly true where strategies and objectives are handed down from above as a fait accompli.

If a consultant interviewed your company's executives and senior managers, one on one, asking about your key strategies and objectives, do you think there would be a lot of consensus?

Strategies and objectives are items you do not want to leave open to interpretation, but this can happen if the directives are too abstract. Ambiguity in the descriptions of strategies and objectives can cause confusion. Language itself can often contribute to it. Unclear or abstract language can compromise or delay the organization's ability to execute and achieve the desired results. For example, a directive at a nuclear power plant once read, "You cannot put too much liquid coolant into the reactor core's cooling system." While most would interpret this to mean "Don't put too much coolant in," wouldn't you hate to live through the consequences of someone misunderstanding the note to mean "There is no limit to how much coolant you can put in"? You'd be astounded at some of the ambiguities found in mission statements and strategic briefs.

The solution is to involve executives and senior managers in the formulation of those plans. Outside facilitators are sometimes engaged because they can act dispassionately and preserve objectivity. In the end, though, before the game plan is transmitted to the "troops," the team that put it together should review and refine it to the point of full team consensus. This may seem obvious, but again many companies discover differences in view only after they see the "official" document.

Agile companies are more likely to include cross-functional participation in strategic development. And they do it not only to foster feelings of inclusion but because they believe that a variety of perspectives helps to avoid myopic decisions.

PEOPLE WHO BUY INTO THE STRATEGY AND OBJECTIVES

What would you prefer, great strategy and so-so execution or so-so strategy with great execution?

For Carl Vogel of Charter Communications it's a "no-brainer." He'd opt for the latter every time. When Vogel worked for Glenn Jones, founder of Jones Intercable and a cable operator pioneer, the first strategy was aimed at acquiring 50,000 subscribers though Jones' vision was to get three million subscribers. "The strategy stayed the same," said Vogel, "and Glenn just kept raising the bar each time." Later, when Vogel left cable to work in direct broadcast satellites, he and his boss watched their multimillion-dollar satellite being launched on closed-circuit TV. Everything looked great until, a minute later, the rocket and satellite blew up. In the spectrum of bad days at the office, this one definitely pushed the needle. At that point, the company had 60 days to put a satellite in place or go bust. "The strategy was very quick," said Vogel. "Charlie (his boss) said, 'I'll find a rocket, you find the money, and we'll meet back here in a month.'" His boss found a rocket, Vogel made some crucial deals, and total disaster was averted. The execution was flawless. That's performance.

After its $17 billion acquisition of General Instrument Company, a major set-top box manufacturer, Motorola tapped that company's CEO, Ed Breen, as its president and chief operating officer. Breen's first assignment was to integrate the staff and products of the two companies within six months. He did it in one. His prescription was "first know strategically where you want to head." From there it's:

❑ Lay out the strategic blueprint,
❑ Communicate it constantly, and
❑ Act on it.

In a merger like that one, Breen says, people want to know where they stand. If you keep people in the dark, things can slow down. "It's much better to take action quickly, be decisive, and get things out of the way."

SKILLS NEEDS CAN CHANGE

When Terry McGraw first took the helm at McGraw-Hill, he said, "I looked at management and I didn't think I had the ability with that group to do what I think needed to be done. So, I decided to make changes." Using a baseball analogy, McGraw said, "To do what I wanted, I needed several hitters with .300 batting averages. And I just didn't have that kind of bench strength." There were lots of management changes in 1993 and 1994. "People were saying, 'What's wrong with McGraw? No one gets along with him,'" McGraw admitted. "I have to say, it even gave me pause." But by 1994 and 1995, the company's market capitalization jumped from $2.8 to $4, then to $5 billion. "Then it really took off and hit $14 billion," McGraw smiled. "I knew then that I finally had a performance team in place."

PERFORMANCE TEAM BUILDING

A performance culture is shaped by a performance team; therefore team building is a key prerequisite of agile business. In team building, a team studies its own process of working together and works to establish an environment that encourages and values the contributions of its members. Energies are directed at problem solving, task effectiveness, and optimal use of members' resources to realize the team's objectives. The following are characteristics of good team building:

❑ Interdependence among team members is high
❑ Team leader has good people skills and is committed to team approach
❑ Each team member is willing to contribute
❑ Team develops a relaxed climate for communication
❑ Team members develop a mutual trust
❑ Team and individuals are prepared to take risks
❑ Team is clear about goals and establishes targets
❑ Team member roles are defined

❏ Team members know how to examine team and individual errors without personal attacks

❏ Team has capacity to create new ideas

❏ Each team member knows he or she can influence the team agenda

Agile businesses have their share of very smart people and with that comes the challenge of managing egos. According to Rand Blazer, president and CEO of KPMG Consulting, Inc. in an interview with Regina Fazio Maruca of *Fast Company*, "Don't ask people to set their egos aside for the good of the team. Feed their egos." He recommends giving people areas of responsibility in which to excel. For example, make one member the team's leader of communications, make another the head of technology, and so on. Adds Blazer, " Do these team leaders also have egos that need feeding? Of course. Give those people enough room to roam, to set the agenda for their team's goals, and to maintain their own identity elsewhere in the job. These people are probably senior members of your organization. Make sure you treat them that way."

It takes people to carry out strategic actions. How well they do depends upon their skills and the degree to which they buy into the strategy and objectives. That, in turn, will be driven in part by how included they feel in the development of those strategies and actions and how well upper-level management has sold the strategy to those below.

Good teachers understand that dissemination of information is not the same as teaching, and reciting a bunch of related facts is not the same as learning. Buy-in means internalizing an idea, seeing one's actions as part of a whole that one agrees with. Inclusion is a critical part of achieving buy-in, but the practical issue is how to achieve inclusion and efficiency at the same time.

> Good teachers understand that dissemination of information is not the same as teaching, and reciting a bunch of related facts is not the same as learning.

For example, direct democracy is the most inclusive form of government. First practiced by the Greeks, everyone participated in framing social rules. But representative democracy balances inclusion with efficiency. In the U.S., we directly elect people who, in turn, directly influence legislation. In a large business, certainly, it is impractical to include everyone in all stages of strategic development and objectives, but it makes sense to include at least one representative of all groups in those deliberations. If the people in the trenches feel that one of them was included in all aspects of a plan, they are more likely to believe that their interests have also been served.

There are successive levels of buy-in. The first level is buy-in of the overall strategy and objectives. All involved in execution need to see the big picture, first, and how this strategy makes sense in that context. From there, the next level of buy-in is that objectives are connected to the appropriate set of actions and anticipated results.

Here is often where lower-level input establishes its value. With strategies developed from a top-down perspective, it is easy to gloss over issues that may end up being sticking points. People expected to carry out those actions may raise those issues, now, before the concrete has had a chance to harden. *Reader's Digest* CEO Ryder adopted an approach where employees themselves, or process owners, would come up with the objectives and methods rather than simply weighing in on methods handed down from above.

Even if the input ultimately causes no changes, the person who raised it sees that it has been considered carefully. That is often enough to make that person feel heard and included. Even better, if some alternative can be struck that integrates the original intent and the person's issue, it is viewed as a win-win. For example, Mary Parker Follett, a management theory visionary of the 1920s, talked about conflict resolution in terms of *domination, compromise,* or *integration.*

In the first instance, domination, a leader simply exerts his or her power and forces a decision. With compromise, everyone feels some sense of loss. But with integration, a new decision is synthesized that everyone feels "meets the desires of all parties with no one having to sacrifice." To illustrate the point, Stephen Covey, author of *The Seven Habits of Highly Effective People,* uses a story about one person wanting to open a window for ventilation and another person wanting to close the window to keep the wind from blowing papers around. The integrated solution was to open a window in an adjoining room. The result was ventilation without wind: everybody's needs were met.

MEASUREMENTS THAT LINK OPERATIONS TO STRATEGIES

In a survey, *Achieving Measurable Performance Improvement in a Changing World*, conducted by KPMG involving *Fortune* 1000 and top public-sector executives in the U.S. and Europe, 93% of those surveyed believed that measurement is "very/somewhat" effective in influencing the results of their departments or entities. But only 51% are "very/somewhat" satisfied with their current systems, and only 15% are "very" satisfied. Clearly, something is wrong.

A strategic plan is meaningless unless you have some way of measuring associated factors and linking the measurements to operations and strategic objectives. When measurement systems produce insufficient or

> **About half of the KPMG survey respondents thought their measurement systems were not up to par. Said one, "First, it failed because it was measuring measurable things instead of things that mattered. Second, it failed because it measured too many things."**

inapplicable information, people either are led astray by them or ignore them. About half of the KPMG survey respondents thought their measurement systems were not up to par. Said one, "First, it failed because it was measuring measurable things instead of things that mattered. Second, it failed because it measured too many things."

Professor Göran Roos, an expert in strategy and performance measurement systems, who was quoted in a KPMG white paper describing the survey results, concurred: "Too often measurement systems are driven by what is available rather than what is needed. In my experience the shortcomings are three-fold: 1) management's view is not as commonly held as it appears at first sight; 2) even when organizations are tracking intangibles, they only look at how much they have, not how those intangibles are used; and 3) compromises are made so that the measures actually used do not properly reflect the underlying key success factors."

Panorama Business Views, a performance information software company, describes the problem in a list of seven "deadly sins":

❏ No understanding of a given measure's cause or effect,
❏ Measures that exist solely to reinforce organizational silos,
❏ Measures that blur key issues,
❏ Unreliable or inaccurate data,
❏ Measures that require extensive resources to compile,
❏ Measures that can be "filtered," and
❏ No link between measures and individual performance management.

Many of the executives we interviewed believe performance measurement is essential for aligning their organizations with strategies, and most agreed that implementing an effective performance measurement program is challenging. One reason is such a program creates the kinds of changes that organizations usually resist. Frequently managers oppose the development of performance measures because they consider their work too specialized or qualitative to be accurately measured by some statistic.

Intel's Andy Grove was quoted as saying, "If it can be measured, it can be improved." Sometimes, though, measurement can work against you. Once you establish a measure, use it consistently, let everyone know what's expected and what's resulted, and your people will align with that measure. If it's the "right" set of measures, the organization will align with your strategies and objectives. If it's the "wrong" set, they'll align with a faulty interpretation of the strategies and objectives.

For example, a service company developed a strategy for increasing its profitability. Billings were based on hourly fees and materials charges, so the strategy called for increasing the average amount of billable hours. Before implementing the strategy, the average of billable hours was 76% of total hours. The objective was to raise this average to 85%.

The company succeeded in raising the billable average to 85%, but profitability rose less than 2%. When they did some troubleshooting, they found out why.

The amount actually billed to clients was an adjusted amount based on billable hours and materials. But, in a month where average billable hours was 76%, the amount actually billed was equivalent to only 69%. About 7% was adjusted out due to over-budget situations and billings disputes. When the bar had been raised to 85%, consultants spent more time and billed more hours, but budgetary limitations stayed the same. The 9% increase in average billings simply increased the adjusted percentage by an additional 7%. Thus, the increase to 85% on average produced actual billings equivalent to 71%.

The measurement system failed in several ways. Billable time was batch-loaded, weekly, so consultants had no way of reconciling the hours they were billing and budgetary limits. In addition, materials charges were batch-loaded separately and could trigger write-downs in billable hours by pushing the total above the budget limit. Moreover, consultants did not get net billable results until well after the fact, when it was often too late to seek approval for additional fee hours from the clients. Managers had little choice but to write off those hours.

The new system used online billing and gave consultants real-time information about present billing and budget limits. It also factored in the current materials charges per job. It became clear that existing jobs accounted for an average billability of about 72% to 73%, and that to achieve the 85% percent average, more jobs had to be handled concurrently or fewer consultants had to be handling the current load. At the time, there was a backlog of work that management was holding pending additional hires. By assigning those additional jobs, the billable average rose to 82% and net billings were equivalent to 77.5%. By changing some of the items discussed, the firm was able to increase profitability. In addition, the amount of write-downs decreased significantly, and so did the magnitude of billing disputes. Client satisfaction rose commensurately.

In a broader sense, though, you need to look at what you are measuring to see if it really reflects your levels of performance. Historically, measurement has focused on traditional performance areas—financial, operational, or functional efficiency. These measures tend to be plentiful, quantitative, internally generated, and derived from operational accounting and information systems. They are also like looking at a rear-view mirror. They show you where you've been but not where you're going.

Non-traditional measures, however, are less well defined. They are more intangible, such as market, strategic implementation, and resource management. Such measures have the potential for leading indication, but are often supported by data that is incomplete, anecdotal, and inconsistently gathered.

> Historically, measurement has focused on traditional performance areas—financial, operational, or functional efficiency. These measures tend to be plentiful, quantitative, internally generated, and derived from operational accounting and information systems. They are also like looking at a rear-view mirror.

Yet, if companies are to implement measuring systems that are aligned with and adapted to suit their strategies and business models, they must address both the traditional and non-traditional areas. Strategy is by nature futuristic, and businesses need measurements that show where they are headed. Today, companies are changing their business models and strategies with increasing speed, so the need for better performance measurement systems is growing. And that means systems supported by complete, consistent, and timely data.

REWARD SYSTEMS THAT REINFORCE ALIGNMENT OF ACTIVITIES WITH OBJECTIVES

Used properly, reward systems are ways of compensating, communicating, reinforcing, and aligning. Reward systems are a form of positive reinforcement and, as such, are a most effective tool for encouraging desired behavior. They stimulate people to act because they want to and because they get something of value for doing so.

In Thomas Wilson's *Innovative Reward Systems for the Changing Workplace*, he uses an acronym—SMART—to describe the criteria that underlie an effective reward system:

❑ **Specific:** A line of sight should be maintained between rewards and actions.

❑ **Meaningful:** The achievements rewarded should provide an important return on investment to both the performer and the organization.

❑ **Achievable:** The employee's or group's goals should be within the reach of the performers.

❑ **Reliable:** The program should operate according to its principles and purpose.

❑ **Timely:** The recognition/rewards should be provided frequently enough to make performers feel valued for their efforts.

Reward systems are the way we tie measurements to objectives. It is crucial that all measures be understood by everyone and that a tracking system be in place to monitor performance in the measured areas.

Performance and progress measures must be accessible. They should be displayed in a public area or intranet online portal. Keeping them online makes it easier to keep the data current, which is important. Support systems should be in place to help anyone who wants to try to improve performance.

Celebrate strategic milestones and recognize people who have excelled. But make sure the reward system creates a sense of collective "winning." A system that encourages internal competition can be a very divisive and destructive force.

> Celebrate strategic milestones and recognize people who have excelled. But make sure the reward system creates a sense of collective "winning."

Finally, make sure that rewards are contingent upon results. Reward programs become entitlement programs if they are not tied to results. Every reward should be fully earned, and your people should understand exactly what they have done to achieve it.

PUTTING IT ALL TOGETHER

Agile businesses have performance cultures. There is consensus about strategies and objectives, the right combination of skills is in place, and effective team building has established a motivated performance team.

Through cross-functional participation, they've identified the metrics that reflect their performance objectives. They then make sure that their system can make those measurements, accurately and continuously. Measurement results are openly shared, not as a way to browbeat but as a way to learn and improve.

Reward systems are tied to metrics that are in turn tied to objectives. Rewards are specific, meaningful, achievable, reliable, and timely. Groups and individuals are recognized for their achievements, and collaboration, rather than internal competition, is the motivation.

....

CHAPTER SEVEN

Contrarians at the Gate

Sometimes agile businesses appear to be bucking the trends. They spend when others are trimming budgets, they advertise when others are going quiet, they innovate when competitors are hunkering down, they hire while others fire, and they merge while others purge. It's almost like they have some kind of crystal ball and can see a different future than others see.

Contrary behavior is relative, though, to where things are in the economic cycle. Companies that are hiring like crazy, buying capital equipment, taking on more debt, and spending more on marketing are acting "normally" if we're at the middle of an expansion phase. Doing the same things in the middle of a contraction will label them as "contrarian" at best, "out of control" at worst.

Agile companies are never being contrary for contrary sake. Nor do they follow the herd in mindless fashion. Most times, it looks like they are using the "conventional" playbook. But when their actions seem contrary, it's because they have paid attention to alternatives, and those actions can deliver extraordinary results.

But when their actions seem contrary, it's because they have paid attention to alternatives, and those actions can deliver extraordinary results.

Siebel Systems, for example, was being zealously customer service-oriented in 1998 and 1999 when other companies in the e-business software space were being more standoffish in the glow of mountainous demand. *Business Week* described Siebel as a conservatively managed company "sans flash—buttoned-up and tranquil." But, when the market's demand curve turned down, Siebel's customer loyalty paid off. Those companies that had played hard to get discovered revenues were hard to find. Siebel was not immune to the downturn, but its results were not devastating. Even though its calendar 2002 earnings have suffered along with the rest of the industry, as of May 2002 the stock was still trading at 33 times earnings, compared with a low of 19 in 2001. Few in this business could make a similar claim.

Even before September 11, the airlines were in trouble. A sharp spike in oil prices in 2000 had done its share of damage to earnings and the economic contraction was crippling demand for business travel. Every airline began shedding jobs. Every airline, that is, except Southwest. In its 30-plus year history, Southwest had never had a layoff, and its management looked for cost management alternatives. It found some in delayed delivery of ordered aircraft and was able to reduce costs without reducing headcount. As air travel began to rebound, Southwest had the capacity and people to handle its share. Company morale remained steady, and Southwest was one of the few profitable exceptions in an industry racked by heavy losses.

SPENDING AGAINST THE TIDE

In 1982 unemployment was averaging 9.7%, peaking at 10.8% that November. Inflation floated at just above 6%. Most companies were cutting back, hunkering down, and taking a wait-and-see approach to everything.

3M Corporation, though, chose that time to embark on an ambitious project—standardizing its information technology everywhere in the world. The objective was to have a single IT infrastructure instead of 63 (e.g., one in each country in which it operated).

This wasn't the first time 3M used a bad economy as a backdrop for investment and innovation. It had invented Scotch tape in 1930 and established its Central Research Laboratory in 1937, in the heart of the Great Depression. In bad times "you're forced to be creative and innovative because you have less resources with which to work," explained David Drew, 3M's vice president of IT.

And the benefits of spending against the tide have served 3M well. IT headcount has been kept lower, in fact, 25% lower than in 1982. According to Drew, this has permitted 3M to breeze through the IT worker shortage during much of the dot.com boom. The company's IT budget, now, is only 35% higher than in 1982.

FedEx is another company that has used recession years

and economic slumps as an opportunity to invest and innovate. In 1979 and 1980, FedEx introduced computer systems for managing shipments and coordinating customer pickups. Then, in 1989 and 1991, FedEx established a satellite-based system for locating vehicles and providing centralized routing management. It is using the most recent recession as an opportunity to expand its Web presence, particularly Web customer service technology. Presently more FedEx customers use its Web site rather than its toll-free number. With an average of one million track requests per day, less than 10% are now done using the phone. With every toll-free call costing FedEx $2.14 and each Web inquiry averaging 10 cents, there's real bottom-line payoff in moving customers onto the Web.

With the double whammy of economic contraction and September 11, 2001, travel budgets have been especially hammered affecting airlines, car rentals, and hotels. But in January 2001, Dollar Rent-A-Car invested in an application allowing it to take reservations directly from airline Web sites. The program was launched with Southwest Airlines in May 2001, and Dollar expects it to generate about $10 million in new revenue because, with one click, a Southwest customer can turn into a Dollar customer.

Steve Ellis, managing director at Bain & Co., said, "If you invest during a period of turbulence and you gain strength relative to your competitors during that period, you earn the rights to a disproportionate amount of the growth that will come when the economy rebounds." One pitfall to avoid, according to Ellis, is to tamper with your business model in pursuit of any and all revenue opportunities. It can "fragment and dilute the focus of the organization ... and what its principal value proposition is to its target customer base."

There's logic to investing during fragile times. Adrian Slywotzky, vice president at Mercer Management Consulting, put it this way in an interview with *Fast Company* in March 2002, "Recessions are hell, but they provide unique strategic opportunities. It's very hard to gain relative position in a boom: everybody's paying attention; everybody's focused; everybody's adding capacity; and everybody's spending. Smart companies have demonstrated that it's drastically easier to improve relative position during a downturn."

> "If you invest during a period of turbulence and you gain strength relative to your competitors during that period, you earn the rights to a disproportionate amount of the growth that will come when the economy rebounds."
> —Steve Ellis, Managing Director, Bain & Co.

A BEACON IN THE DARK

One of our upper-management contacts at an analog chipmaker told us that, at the first hint of a downturn, the company instituted a broad and deep cut in advertising and marketing communications budgets. "Our key competitor, though, never missed a beat in its advertising, so it'll be interesting to see how that plays out in the rebound," he lamented.

His concern is rightly placed. As stated earlier, research has shown that companies that maintain or increase advertising during recessions do far better than those that cut back both during the recession and for years afterward. Part of it is brand reinforcement at a time when buyers are particularly risk-averse. And part of it is consistency. When a company has been advertising regularly in the same media, it is conspicuous by its absence should it suddenly stop.

During economic contractions, companies that have not been prudent with their balancing of revenues and costs will have to spread the cost-cutting pain across all areas, advertising included. This, of course, lowers the noise level for those that have been prudent. But even some of those companies will take short-term solace in deep advertising cuts. Agile companies know better.

There was little to celebrate in the semiconductor industry in 2000 and 2001. Sales of technology products were down across the board, and sales of the semiconductor components with which they are made sank, too. That ripple effect from systems to chips carried further into the realm of semiconductor capital equipment. As such, Applied Materials revised its forecasts down. But if anyone thought the company would cut costs, hunker down, and wait to see which way the wind blew, they were mistaken. Applied Materials budgeted $30 million for advertising in 2001, and the bulk of it was earmarked for brand image advertising. The message these ads would carry is Applied Materials makes "the systems used to produce virtually every new microchip in the world."

Certainly, Applied Materials is not the first technology company to spend big bucks on image advertising. Cisco, Intel, Nortel, and others have paved that way before. But few can remember a company whose business is so far removed from consumer mind share and purchasing decisions committing large advertising resources to a mass media campaign. In the case of the "Intel inside" campaign, the objective was to associate PC innovation and quality with Intel microprocessors, and hopefully give pause to purchase decisions of PCs using someone else's chip. This advertising strategy does raise Applied Materials' name recognition among people outside the semiconductor industry and could predispose investors to select that stock when planning to establish positions in the semiconductor sector. The ads do raise awareness of how Applied Materials' products basically touch everything and associates a little known, little understood process into something bigger. From Applied's Morgan's point of view, it's a great time to make the investment because the noise level is so low it automatically enhances the message's impact.

No one would accuse Microsoft of being skittish if it had trimmed advertising in 2001. After all, the technology sector had been so vulnerable and sales of servers, desktops, and laptops were all down. But the company signed off on over $1 billion in advertising in 2001—double its budget for 2000! Branding and brand association have been a staple of Microsoft's strategy for decades, and the company is using the downturn as an opportunity to increase both market and mind share. The value of advertising dollars during economic contractions goes up significantly. First there are the lower prices charged by the print media trying to balance editorial with advertising page count and by the broadcast media attempting to fill advertising time slots. Add to this the overall decrease in messages and message sources and you have the equivalent of talking in a low-noise milieu versus shouting in the midst of an uproar.

INNOVATING INSTEAD OF HIBERNATING

During economic boom times, it's hard to keep up, even conceptually, with the pace of innovation in technology, products, and business models. The contrast during contractions though makes one think of descriptions such as "suspended animation" to paint word images of business energy levels. We don't expect revolutionary changes during business downturns, and most industries do not surprise us. Even evolutionary change comes at a much slower pace, but it does come. Agile businesses take advantage of the competitive respite to ratchet up their competitive advantages through evolutionary innovation.

Take Reuters, for example. It is leveraging the "quiet" of the 2002 downturn to make a very loud splash at two of the world's largest, most visible sporting events, the Winter Olympics and the World Cup. In Salt Lake, for example, the company deployed its new, state-of-the-art wireless delivery system, an operation that allowed Reuters journalists and photographers, spread over 12 different and climatically challenging geographic areas, to transmit news and pictures instantly everywhere—not bad when you consider that the ideal photo location for downhill skiing is halfway up the mountain where the average daily low is minus 62 degrees Fahrenheit! Pleased with the positive exposure garnered from that event, Reuters performed a similar feat at the 2002 Korea/Japan World Cup, when it used yet another high-visibility setting to launch what the company feels is its most comprehensive multimedia package ever. The two programs are evidence of CEO Tom Glocer's instincts in taking advantage of the competitive lull. That's agility.

Recessions, in fact, are a time when some companies and even industries make major changes in strategic direction. Doug Henton, founder and president of the Silicon Valley-based firm of Collaborative Economics, points to 1970 as a key turning point in the semiconductor industry. Until then, a substantial share of integrated circuits (ICs) were sold to military systems and avionics companies. Afterward, the industry focused much more on business and consumer electronics because the military market had become much too volatile.

In the early 1970s, U.S. memory chipmakers were world leaders and major market shareholders. A subsequent downturn saw the U.S. companies waiting and holding while their Japanese competitors sunk big bucks in advanced R&D. When the upturn came, Japanese memory chip vendors had leapfrogged their U.S. counterparts. Intel had been a dynamic RAM chip pioneer, but as those products became commodity priced, Intel focused on higher margin memories, such as erasable PROMs (EPROMs) and electrically erasable PROMs (EEPROMs). During the recession in the mid-1980s, though, Intel focused its innovations on microprocessors and never looked back. The symbiosis between Intel's microprocessors and PC innovation and market growth transformed the company into today's powerhouse.

Even the recession of the early 1990s was the incubator for what would become the Internet and dot.com innovations that exploded from 1995 through 2000. It's still too early to say which innovations cloaked in the recession of 2001 will set new milestones and benchmarks in the expansion phase that follows. But you can be sure that whatever is moving mountains at the outset of the next expansion was developed during the dark days of the recession that preceded it.

HIRING DURING THE SLUMP

In a study by researchers from Creighton University, Oklahoma State University, and Texas Christian University, reported in June 2001, companies that swam against the current and hired key managers and professionals during an economic downturn showed stronger financial performance.

Companies that swam against the current and hired key managers and professionals during an economic downturn showed stronger financial performance.

Said lead researcher, Charles Greer, associate dean for graduate programs in the Neeley School of Business at Texas Christian, "This is the first empirical study to show that using contrarian financial investment strategy, of going against the herd and hiring a few key personnel during a downturn, results in stronger financial performance two years later." The researchers also found that "those companies less willing to incur the risk of investing in their human resources during economic downturns achieved lower financial returns after the downturn."

You don't have to be a big company to apply this contrarian strategy. CapTech Ventures, based in Richmond, Virginia, provides information technology services and customized Internet-based applications. The company competes in one of the hardest-hit sectors of the tech economy—interactive media—so no one would have blamed CEO Sandy Williamson if he took a conservative, conventional approach in 2001, cutting staff, canceling product rollouts, or selling off lines of business to save on overhead. Instead, Williamson opted to stick with the pre-recession plan, which meant shooting for a 34% revenue gain, while tripling the advertising and marketing budget and increasing headcount by 16%.

The company's full-time staff grew from 50 to 58 as Williamson carried through on the plan. And others concurred with his strategy. Said Robert J. Stolle, executive director of the Greater Richmond Technology Council, "Companies that are hiring now recognize that in six months or so they won't be able to touch these people, because they'll be gobbled up by competitors."

During 1999, human resource management was a high-stress profession. The total number of open positions frequently outnumbered the total number of all applicants. Competitors were offering signing bonuses, quick vesting stock options, unpublicized perquisites, moving expenses, and all sorts of creative attractants. It was nothing less than people resource inflation, driven by increasing demand and dwindling supply.

The sudden and deep downturn had a sobering effect on employers and employees. Often, senior managers who jumped from relatively secure positions in mature companies, tantalized by the seemingly endless expansion of dot.com market capitalization, found themselves out of work with nowhere to go. And with each new bankruptcy, the situation only got worse.

The downturn churned up a lot of suddenly available talent, and today's human resource department typically has far more applicants than openings. The shock of the downturn and its upheaval persists. Job aspirants are looking at a lot more than compensation. They are asking hard questions and listening carefully to the answers. For their part, employers are also asking tougher questions, especially with the intense pressure to fill gaping holes now lifted.

Agile businesses use recessions as people resource opportunities. Instead of intense competition over high-priced and scarce talent, there's a larger talent pool with fewer fishing lines in the water. There are also more engagement options to choose from. It's a buyer's market in a recession and talent can be hired without employers being gouged.

One of the advantages of hiring during a recession is you can take more time and, hopefully, make better choices. Another is you have more opportunity to train people without the press of frantic production requirements. Several of the CEOs we interviewed said this is a great time to "hire rookies" and bring them along while the most experienced people have time for them.

OPPORTUNITIES TO ACQUIRE OR MERGE

Recessions have a way of shaking talent loose and dramatically increasing the opportunities to acquire and/or merge. Propositions that would have been dismissed out of hand during the boom phase quickly become topics for serious consideration during recessions. During heady times, companies, divisions, and intellectual properties are priced like rare gems if available at all. In the midst of a downturn, though, "for sale" signs go up and prices come down.

What had formerly been a seller's market is rapidly transformed into a buyer's market. But this is no time to lower the "buyer beware" radar or give due diligence short shrift. Agile businesses recognize that recessions can be a time rife with acquisition possibilities, but they also approach them with a consistent set of best practices and unwavering discipline that does not change with the economic cycle.

Edward D. Breen, CEO of General Instrument, when it was acquired by Motorola in January 2000, merged the two companies' broadband and network-equipment operations. And he did in one month what he had been given six months to accomplish. But the hidden preparation took place months before the official marriage. Both organizations were deeply involved in managing the merger, defining clear objectives, and formulating a merger plan.

Cisco became quite proficient in merging acquired companies. Said Shaun Kelly, partner in charge of KPMG's America's Transactions Services, "Cisco has a whole process in place. The day after the acquisition closes, people in an acquired company were clear on benefits, who they report to, and so on. People going through the change curve are often disillusioned and can become unproductive. Cisco puts integration folks in the process right away."

Several of those interviewed agreed that most merger problems stem from underestimating the effort to blend corporate cultures. Said one, "Computer incompatibilities can be overcome; cultural incompatibilities are fatal." One of the factors that can confound cultural melding is an acquirer's desire to subsume an acquired company's distinct brand under its own master brand.

One of the factors that can confound cultural melding is an acquirer's desire to subsume an acquired company's distinct brand under its own master brand.

Despite the immense popularity of mergers and acquisitions (M&As) during 1998 and 1999, many "deals" failed to live up to expectations. The reasons included paying too high a price; underestimating the time, costs, and difficulties involved in melding the two company cultures; and overestimating the value to be gained by merging two organizations. Eight of the 10 biggest M&A deals of all time took place in 1998. Worldwide, more than 23,000 deals took place that year, accounting for $2.5 trillion worth of transactions. And during the first two quarters of 1999, another $1.5 trillion worth of M&A transactions had taken place.

In the surveys and analyses done by KPMG, the following were the primary deal drivers behind M&As, large and small:

❑ Added growth prospects,
❑ Acquisition of strategic assets (e.g. technology),
❑ Reduced overall selling, general, and administrative (SG&A) costs,
❑ Reduced future capital expenditures,
❑ Enhanced gross margins,
❑ More efficient use of working capital,
❑ Enhanced image in the investment community,
❑ One-time cash creation (e.g., by selling idle assets or non-core divisions),
❑ Lowered borrowing costs, and
❑ Tax-related savings or efficiencies.

About 75% of those surveyed believed their deal had been successful in achieving the objectives, but the stated objectives varied considerably. To test how closely perception correlated with reality, the survey team used a relative measure of equity-price change—taken before an M&A transaction, then taken again a year after the deal was concluded. Remember: three-quarters of the main board of directors had perceived their transactions as successful. But the first survey completed in 1999 showed that, in fact, more than half the deals destroyed value, nearly a third changed nothing, and only 17% of the deals resulted in adding value.

A second survey completed in 2001 was more optimistic. Lost-value transactions were now down to 31% and those adding value had risen to 30%. But one disturbing statistic showed that the plurality (39%) had made essentially no difference. There was no relationship between the number of M&A transactions a company completed and its likelihood of success. But, based on the drop in failures and rise in successes in 2001 compared with 1999, more M&As were adding to shareholder value. The question is, "Is this a trend or an anomaly?"

If the economic cycle had not shifted, we believe that the success rate would indeed have continued to improve. Companies were getting better at making good deals. But with the upheaval in market capitalization and a worldwide downturn, assessing prospective deals required different benchmarks and possibly different skills.

Done well, M&As can add significant value. The KPMG team did identify certain key practices that affected the successful outcome of a transaction. They were:

❑ Early action,
❑ Main board leadership,
❑ Pre-bid value assessment,
❑ Formal transaction process plan,
❑ End-to-end process manager involvement, and
❑ Independent post-deal assessment.

Those companies that used all the practices created shareholder value nearly 70% of the time. Those that applied five practices were successful in adding shareholder value only 36% of the time. And those that employed four or less had an 18% record of success. In addition, timing counted. Those that instituted the practices sooner in the process were more likely to achieve their objectives. And as we said earlier, these factors would appear to be largely independent of where we are in an economic cycle. Practiced consistently regardless of economic phase, they should improve the odds of M&A creating shareholder value.

THEY HAVE NO CRYSTAL BALL!

At times, agile businesses seem to have uncanny prescience. Can they really predict the future? Not really. Chances are, though, that agile businesses are better than competitors at identifying and capturing early-warning signals and making the necessary rapid adaptations.

Calculating Probabilities

Casino owners have no way of knowing if a blackjack player is going to win or lose money while playing a few dozen hands. What they do know is that, over time, because of the casino's blackjack rules, the casino will win more money than it will lose. They don't know what you'll throw in six throws of a die, but they know that you'll throw any particular number about 1,666 times if you roll a die 10,000 times. Calculating probabilities in this case is routine. There are only six different result possibilities and each is equally likely. With a large number of trials, each number will come up one-sixth of the time.

But markets are not dice. And schemes aimed at predicting the trends in the securities market do not apply here. We're talking about real demand, real supply, real costs, real revenues, and real earnings or real losses. This isn't about gambling; it's about strategic moves and calculated risks. For example, even during the economic contraction, online sales totals are continuing to increase. This bodes well for e-commerce, doesn't it? However, surveys show that consumers are more concerned about surveillance online than through other media. Jeffrey Eisenach, president of The Progress and Freedom Foundation, said the U.S. "was already on a 20-year path to being a surveillance society." He believes the privacy wall that has always been there has "been breached (in the course of the aftermath of September 11) and pervasive online surveillance is now a permanent fact of life." But who can predict to what extent that concern about surveillance will affect e-commerce?

In another example, if demand for cell phones is increasing at an average rate of 4% per month for the last 12 months and company ABC is the sole supplier of a chip used in 75% of all cell phones, isn't it a good bet that demand for ABC's chip will continue to increase at least in the short-term (the next six months, say)? This is deterministic, isn't it? There's a calculable probability, here, right? However, what if company DEF announces a pin-compatible component with better specifications and a 15% lower price? What happens to probability, then? The determinism metamorphoses into chaos. And so long as the elements of the free market and the freedom to compete and innovate remain unhampered, market uncertainties will abound in the short term.

At first glance, we're left with the reality that short-term predictability is subject to surprises and uncertainties. What about long-term predictability? Who hasn't heard the dictum that, over the long term, investments in securities will provide higher returns than any other investment? Well, while this is mostly the case, there have been long stretches of time where other investments have produced higher returns. Here, it depends on whether you see the long-term market model as deterministic or chaotic. The short-term market can be either, but all you can really say is that it has been deterministic or chaotic for the last six months but not whether it will continue to be one or the other for the next six months. The same is true for the long-term market. We have 20-20 hindsight about its nature, but lots of uncertainty about its future.

Predicting Gets Harder the Farther Out You Look

In weather forecasting, we have a lot of things going for us. We have satellites that can look down at virtually every corner of the planet. We have instrumentation recording temperatures, pressures, and wind speeds. Yet, when it comes to accuracy in four-day forecasting, our batting average is not good. It gets better with a one-day forecast, but goes downhill beyond that. Weather is the quintessential chaotic system.

With markets, we have abundant measurements, too. Unlike weather forecasting, though, our information reflects the past, not the present. We can monitor money supply, unemployment, international trade dynamics, currency movement, and more. But our information is weeks and often months old. So, we never have a clear present view, just a fleeting rear-view mirror perspective. It is impossible without significant uncertainty to gauge a market's future behav-

Frankly, even five-*month* plans are shaky. And the more volatility a market has shown in recent weeks, the more uncertain short-term plans become.

ior, and the uncertainty grows by leaps and bounds as we try to push those forecasts further out. The five-year plans that industries adopted in the 1950s and 1960s would be absolutely ludicrous in 2001. Frankly, even five-*month* plans are shaky. And the more volatility a market has shown in recent weeks, the more uncertain short-term plans become.

Lessons from NASA—Build in Mid-Course Corrections

So, agile businesses apply rocket science to their plans and strategies. Despite the incredible precision of NASA computers, plus accurate position and velocity data for the Earth and the Moon, it would be nearly impossible to plot a fixed course and land a rocket on the Moon. Instead, NASA plots a course that can be incrementally adjusted from the time the rocket blasts off until it touches down on the lunar surface.

Agile businesses take a similar tack with their business plans and strategies. They plot a course that can also be incrementally adjusted, and adjustments are influenced by pertinent data gathered, processed, and distributed continuously to the people who will make those corrections.

One morning in February 2001, Tom Siebel began his morning ritual of reviewing his sales force's quarterly forecast. What he saw made him sit up straight. Hundreds of deals from a couple of thousand to millions of dollars appeared

stalled. And individual sales reports cited budget elimina-
tions, frozen IT spending, and decision deferrals. To Siebel the
implications were clear—the onset of a crash was at hand.

Just hours later Siebel met with six senior executives,
telling them what he saw, how he interpreted it, and asking for
a major rethinking of the company's 2001 growth strategy—a
strategy that had been "finalized" only a few weeks before.
Meanwhile, he made sure his executive team would visit key
customers and close pending deals right away, he himself visiting nine of them.

Siebel gets credit for being one of the first to see and warn
about an impending technology downturn. More important,
he acted quickly upon what he saw. "Tom instruments (e.g.,
puts in place ways of measuring) his business better than anyone I've ever seen, and he manages accordingly," said Robert
Austrian, an analyst at Banc of America Securities. "He was
way ahead in seeing the downturn, and he put the screeching
brakes on."

But Siebel did more than stomp on the brake pedal; he
also made significant adjustments to the strategy. The three
driving goals became making sure customers are happy and
remain happy, keeping cash flowing in, and protecting market share. Part of any agile business's plan is having contingencies and alternatives ready to deploy in advance of need.
When it's done well, it all looks seamless and cohesive. And,
sometimes, it looks downright contrarian.

....

CHAPTER EIGHT

It's Not Easy Being Lean

E ffective cost management has been a core requirement of businesses at all times. Hundreds of books have been written about the subject and it is not our intention here to make any claims of improving on them. It has been our observation, however, that when demand and revenues are waning, the tendency to retrench causes many companies to approach cost management reflexively. Yet, as we have learned from Jim Morgan, "Great companies are built in tough times." Through companies like Applied, we've seen that innovation and creativity can be applied with the same discipline to costs as they can to product creation and development, with excellent and often unexpected results.

CONTORTIONISTS AND CONTRACTION

Contortionism, as such, is not regularly featured in business school curricula. Yet, during times of contraction, leaders in business might be inclined to recall the trials of Harry Houdini who, trussed like a chicken and suspended upside

down in a padlocked tank of water, faced the joint imperatives of freeing the knots that bound him while planning his
successful emergence topside. Despite spawning a mouthful
of clichés about one's world being turned upside down, being
over one's head, having one's hands tied and having no room
to breathe, the business school lesson remains—how to keep
afloat when the tide is against you.

One of the hardest parts to bear in a downturn is the
uncertainty. If one knew when the market would pick-up
again, why then it would be so much easier to plan where and
how to cut and where and how to grow. But reality is not like
that. And people respond differently.

A recent study by Bain Consulting for the *Harvard
Business Review* showed that in the face of impending recession, there were three types of managers. The first type was
overconfident and under-responded. The second type was
under-confident and overresponded. The third type managed
to get the balance just about right.

Of the first group, the study's author said, "Just as most
people on the road assume that they're above-average drivers,
most executives feel that their company will do better than their
competitors when faced with a decline in demand." It takes
longer for leaders in this category to believe that recession is
upon them. Some may feel that analyst reports predicting slower growth are overblown, and others that their businesses are
simply more impervious to volatility than their competitors.
Even those who see the first gray shadows of a down-market
approach may "radiate confidence—and even clairvoyance" so

One CEO we interviewed said, "The biggest mistake that companies have made is to believe that their business is somehow immune from change on the downside.

as not to worry their staff, which they fear might only make things worse. Overly buoyed, these leaders unwittingly expose their companies to the economic undertow.

One CEO we interviewed said, "The biggest mistake that companies have made is to believe that their business is somehow immune from change on the downside. They don't prepare themselves internally, or their people psychologically. So, when it happens, credibility suffers."

The under-confident, over-responders aren't much better. In their attempts to preemptively batten down the hatches, they may dive into non-core businesses to balance what they see as a weaker current lineup. While individual investors may be wise to embrace a diversified portfolio, businesses in the throes of a contraction can do themselves more harm than good by expanding beyond their competencies, for such can have a diluting effect in terms of market share, energy, and resources, the combined result of which may subject the business to more market volatility, not less. These same over-responders are also likely to be seen walking the halls sporting a hatchet and a box of band-aids, an ineffectual pairing at the best of times. The risk here is that while short-term survival may be secured, long-term sustainability may be imperiled.

Instead, leaders who keep one eye firmly on the recovery while "relentlessly managing costs in good times and bad" will be best poised to ride the curves of the downturn and come out ahead at the end.

TRIMMING, SHAVING, PARING

Cutbacks are virtually inevitable in a downturn. In certain sectors, the analyst hue and cry alone makes it a requirement. Yet, the response for many is formulaic. We know the classics—reduce headcount, eliminate perks, trim nonessential services, scale back R&D and production, close plants, slash marketing, and cancel advertising. This is the menu, more or less, and many companies work their way through it from hors d'oeuvres to dessert. If really cash-starved, some will go back and repeat. But as you would expect, too much of this and these same companies will find themselves struggling to get up and move when it's time to go.

Al Dunlap, the former head of Sunbeam, acquired the nickname "Chainsaw Al" for his ruthless approach to slicing costs. It was an approach that later came back to haunt him and his company. Deliberation and care are virtues at all times, but particularly when it comes to pruning an organization. Mercer Management Consulting conducted a study on cost cutting in which it analyzed the performance of 800 companies across different industries over the five-year span of 1987–1992, a period that included the last recession. Of the 120 companies that Mercer had identified as "cost-cutters," the study found that only one in three had achieved profitable revenue growth in the five years following the recession. When the researchers looked for a reason to explain why the remaining two-thirds

> **When the researchers looked for a reason to explain why the remaining two-thirds performed so badly, they discovered that the primary cause was the group's inattention to managing for growth.**

performed so badly, they discovered that the primary cause was the group's inattention to managing for growth. While making cuts, they failed to plan for the rebound. When the market recovered, their more foresighted competitors leapt in front.

In setting the stage for cuts, there are four things to keep in mind.

Cutting Guidelines

1. Don't expect business to return as it was even when the recovery begins. It won't.

2. Recognize that the effects of cuts take time to permeate.

3. Acknowledging the first two points, make cost-cutting an embedded cultural discipline.

4. Do not, in one's pessimism and concern, neglect to plan for growth.

Remember: every cut is a peel-back of a prior investment, so before unsheathing the knife, reflect on the challenges of restitching the pieces when things pick up again. Take plant closings. Companies that pull out of a regional market may end up with the reputation of abandoning their customer base, being fickle, alienating a community. If the company thinks it might possibly return at some future time, it may still want or need to shut down, but will need to take extra care in communicating the planned action. Otherwise, according to one specialist on the topic, "If they return when the economic situation improves, not only are they likely to receive a frosty reaction, but all the work they did in the past to establish a presence will have been lost."

ACROSS THE BOARD CUT

This type of straight cut is tempting to make and seems fair— "Everyone, trim your budgets by 10%." But with an overall cut, a company may be eliminating its best resources, its best products, and its best assets. Look at inventory, for example. Many semiconductor companies carefully monitor their chip stockpiles. These cyclical veterans understand that an overall cut in inventory could mean trimming their best-selling items, exposing them not only to the seasonal dip in sales, but to the wrath of customers frustrated by the company's subsequent inability to deliver its most popular chips on time. Even executives who may understand the imperfections of the straight cut may still be inclined to mandate quotas and percentages. From a management perspective, it is expedient, it is easy to explain internally and externally, and it is easy to monitor. Quite simply, it is less complicated to go to the Street and explain a straight 5% or 10% cut to a hungry group of analysts than it is to talk through a cut of $3\,{}^2/_5\%$.

In our litigious age, the evenness of "across the board" and "last in, first out" measures make them particularly popular when it comes to employee layoffs. But the lack of discretion implicit in such approaches means that the great

In our litigious age, the evenness of "across the board" and "last in, first out" measures make them particularly popular when it comes to employee layoffs. young staffer, your savvy recruiter wooed away from a rival last year, is pink-slipped along with the average-performing engineer who has been with the company for six years. Voluntary retirement offers are similarly flawed, since they likewise leave no room for managerial discernment. Instead, once out there, management is left in a position of waiting and hoping, waiting to see who will accept the package and hoping that they are the right ones.

Many companies have centralized core departments, combining support functions that used to service individual products or divisions into groups that now support several. Such consolidation brings great benefits. It can be easier for these companies to attract senior talent, stimulated at the prospect of managing a larger budget and staff pool. It can help a company in negotiating better vendor terms as well as facilitate better cross-communication among other departments. The complication is that these centralized and frequently quite large groups can become detached from the products or clients they were meant to serve. In the process, brand orientation can get lost. Such brand dilution is one of the risks companies face in making a sweeping move toward centralization. In this way, centralization can work against a company, mitigating the effect of operational efficiencies it might otherwise achieve.

The other real danger is that the weakened focus that

often results makes companies more vulnerable to across-the-board cuts. One publishing company completed a deep restructuring in which it consolidated several departments, such as art and graphics, to serve several titles instead of just one or two. Later, the corporate art director was able to respond readily to a request of a 10% across-the-board reduction, saying, "Sure, I'll cut back." Because he didn't feel as personally connected, he failed to give the decision due consideration. The implications were that the department became "desensitized to the individual brands and titles and their needs, which ultimately resulted in a lack of reader focus," says Frank McGill, partner at magazine consultant Netburn McGill LLC, who observed the fallout.

A CUT TOO FAR

Payroll and benefits costs are one of the largest expense categories for most companies. Eliminating staff—though not pleasant, not easy, and not inexpensive—can nonetheless be accomplished quickly, much faster than, say, divesting oneself of an entire division. Thus, it is easy to see why it makes such a tempting target, so much so that some companies may make multiple waves of staff reductions during a single down-cycle. The short-lived benefits

> The short-lived benefits often give way to long-term headaches, as a company becomes too lean to operate effectively in the rebound.

often give way to long-term headaches, as a company becomes too lean to operate effectively in the rebound.

The American Management Association did a study during the last mild recession in 1992. Their research determined that 60% of the companies that laid off employees in 1992 also laid off employees in 1993. In 1994, the AMA study showed that "two-thirds of the companies that laid off also reported hiring new employees in other areas. When you combine this with the Wyatt Co. finding that most laid-off positions are filled within two years, a binge-and-purge picture begins to emerge. With a watchful eye to quarterly results, company management opens and closes the hiring gate according to short-term financials, not long-term business needs." Arthur D. Little vice president, Peter Vajta, agrees. He believes that the same costs tend to sneak back in. "We've seen situations where there has been almost a one-for-one replacement of the people let go through the hiring of part-time workers, temporaries, and consultants. As a result, the costs don't really disappear. They simply get shifted." Whether it's anorexia, as some conclude, or a binge-and-purge disorder, as the AMA's research indicates, the absence of a sustainable strategy is clearly serious and unhealthy.

There are many legitimate reasons to lay off workers—global competition, technological change, obsolete products and (by extension) workers, flattened organizational hierarchies, and the need to meet investors' profit expectations. If layoffs are part of a broader strategic move, they can have a positive long-term effect. For example, Sears, Roebuck and Co. decided in January 2002 to exit the carpet business. Although 1500 sales jobs will be lost as a consequence, the move is part of a larger effort by Sears' new CEO, Alan Lacy, to refocus the company on its core profit-making divisions. The divestiture of plant and employees made tremendous sense as part of a cohesive plan to phase out a product line.

The primary challenge in managing an employee reduction is ensuring that you are, in fact, laying off the right people. Even if done well, says the *Economist Magazine*, "a bout of layoffs can leave a company traumatized and unfocused" and remaining staff can experience "survivor guilt." Morale takes a hit. Workers can feel less valuable, less motivated, less inclined to be innovative, all of which can impact negatively on productivity. A study by 45 American hospitals conducted in 1998 found that executives who fired someone were two times more likely to suffer a heart attack. Aside from productivity issues, the firing and hiring cycle is also expensive. Recruiting for even junior level staff can cost upwards of $40,000, on top of which there is training and learning lag time. The bottom line is that bottom-line benefits from layoffs may be tempered.

The brokerage firm Edward Jones ranked number one in *Fortune* Magazine's 2002 listing of the "100 Best Companies to Work For." In applying their ranking, *Fortune* commented that, despite the bear market, Edward Jones had laid off no employees and, in fact, had paid bonuses to brokers a week early to make up for the weaker trading climate. This stands in contrast to Edward Jones' fellow St. Louis-based rival A.G. Edwards, which, though ranking 67th on the same list, recently announced an 8% workforce reduction and pay freezes. After Edward Jones made the list the first time in 1998, employment inquiries tripled. Now that it's in the number-one spot, one can surmise that the company will be in the catbird seat when it comes to selecting top applicants.

FedEx and Harley-Davidson also have well-known "no-layoff" philosophies. Companies such as these hope that by adopting such values they may nurture a highly loyal and productive workforce, which they hope will translate to higher customer satisfaction and better bottom-line results. As Greg Rossiter, spokesman for FedEx, says, "We feel we'll be extremely well positioned when the economy does turn up, because we'll reap the benefits of morale …. What differentiates a company in any services industry is its people, and we simply can't afford to put that at risk."

For companies evaluating headcount reductions, here are some points to consider.

Layoff Considerations

Ensure that the layoff is linked to a broader growth strategy. Costs are predictable. Revenues are not. Therefore, we tend to do a better job planning for cuts than for growth. It's important to get the two in sync. Avoid arbitrary headcount reductions.

Develop appropriate performance metrics. Look at the number of management layers, the ratio of exempt to non-exempt employees, direct to indirect labor, and, what some consider the most important metric, the relative cost to manage (management costs as a percentage of total payroll).

Examine alternatives for cost and benefit. For example, where staff reductions will involve sizeable severance packages, some companies may do better restricting overtime or the hours of certain hourly workers. Charter Communications took the innovative approach of reshuffling some of its sales staff, who were less busy in the slow market, to shore up customer service, with the double win of aiding customer retention activities and keeping productivity up.

Engage the help of other departments. For example, companies that face the prospect of a reduced workforce may not realize that their own tax departments can help ease immediate cash-flow problems that can arise in times of contraction. Creative ideas include the possible restructuring of a company's benefits plans in a manner that can help free up cash for other purposes.

SAVINGS MAY BE RIGHT IN FRONT OF YOU

Research shows that when people are under stress they tend to close their minds to new ideas. But, as Garry McGuire, the CFO of Avaya Communications, said, "You need to balance creativity versus controls and process." While the costs associated with basic business functions are a necessary part of doing business, the more successful companies are finding innovative ways to manage these costs and boost their bottom line. Many resourceful ideas abound, but here are a few overlooked areas that most companies, regardless of size, can fairly readily examine and implement.

Business Travel

After payroll and IT, business travel expenses are often shown as the third-largest expense category for most companies. As a result, many are quick to implement travel freezes in the face of a downturn, but opportunities exist for controlling travel costs without placing a potentially harmful ban. Most multinationals have sophisticated travel management functions that offer the threefold benefit of buying power, industry knowledge, and business credit cards with automated systems for capturing and monitoring travel expense data. For those that do not, often small to mid-size companies, acquiring this triptych is worth considering and not as onerous as one might think. Many international travel organizations, such as American Express and Carlson Wagonlit, can effectively outsource the entire function. The potential savings may make it worthwhile.

Take cash advances, for example. American Express research shows that for the average company, administrative processing results in a typical cost of $9 for each cash advance. By standardizing on one corporate credit card for employees who travel, the administrative savings alone can lower the average administrative processing cost to about $1.50.

Procurement

Procurement is another frequently overlooked category. Left to grow organically, many businesses will spawn multiple purchasing organizations that function independently and redundantly. Ad-hoc processes, poorly coordinated information, and the failure to leverage their combined buying strength to pre-negotiate favorable pricing combines in too much being spent on goods and services.

One way to reduce these inefficiencies is through technology. There are a wealth of compelling electronic procurement options in the marketplace. At its simplest, by giving employees access to online catalogs from approved vendors, with products at pre-negotiated prices, they allow employees to make purchases directly from their desktops. Formal procurement software routes such orders automatically through an electronic approval process with real-time tracking along the entire procurement chain. Such streamlining can significantly increase cost savings, in some cases upwards of 5% to 20% of purchased items. Some large companies are beginning to take notice. Amtrak, AstraZeneca, and 3M have all recently contracted with Ariba, a leading developer of automated procurement and "spend management" solutions, to help increase procurement efficiencies, leverage company spending, and reduce costs.

Utilities

Another relatively simple way to save money while also being a good environmentalist is by examining your company's energy needs. We're not talking about installing solar panels or exchanging wool sweaters for the traditional corporate sweatshirt. The fact is that energy expenditures are not often considered when it comes to squeezing out additional costs. But by analyzing historical operating expenses and capital expenditures for energy, companies can negotiate alternative utility rates and establish more predictable energy costs that offer the additional benefit of protecting them against surging prices.

The same logic applies to other utilities like telephone services. Delving through telecommunications vendors' contracts may not be the most glamorous task, but comparing billing rates and invoices may open up opportunities to negotiate better terms with inter-exchange carrier services. From our experience in helping clients in this area, bottom-line savings can range from 15%-40% of a client's gross inter-exchange expense within one year. That's money that can be reinvested in the business.

Real Estate

Real estate can offer other resourceful avenues. The idea is to approach your real estate investment from the standpoint of aligning your current space requirements with your current spending patterns. When locked into a long-term lease signed when your company was growing at 34% a year, this may seem to leave few options. But viewing one's options as limited is anathema to agile businesses. Agile companies try to leverage as much value as possible from their real estate holdings. They examine ways that will lower occupancy cost. They look at options for restructuring their investments in a way that will minimize their tax burden, and they consider opportunities that would turn their holdings into an immediate cash source, through leasebacks, subleasing, or other methods.

Barter

Barter is amongst the oldest forms of trade. At one point in history, even venerable Harvard University engaged in it, by accepting payment of one cow in exchange for tuition. Though it has since occasionally suffered the opprobrium of the business community, which has viewed it as a lowly form of trade, barter witnessed a resurgence during the 1980s and 1990s and was particularly popular with young dot.coms that eagerly exchanged Web advertising space for needed services.

Although bartering is not usually a revenue-generating strategy, it is a cash-saving one and can be a big help for companies that need to preserve scarce dollars. In one case, a small Arizona maker of Internet-enabled directory software, DirXon, managed to thrive in its first year of operations despite launching in what most would have seen as an inopportune time, February 2001. It did so, according to *The Business Journal*, "without leasing office space, hiring a full-time sales force or spending large amounts on branding." Instead, the company relied on bartering exchanges with three other local start-ups, each of whom provide complementary services to the others.

Indirect marketing is an additional benefit of barter, with partners serving as references or word-of-mouth advocates. Such exchanges can also serve as a means of efficiently offloading extra inventory. For those companies where it makes sense, bartering may provide helpful cash relief.

Tax

In the best of times, tax implications are a key component in most business decisions. More and more, the tax department is viewed as an active *profit center*—boosting the bottom line by structuring business undertakings in the most tax-efficient manner. Although companies recognize that their tax departments can make significant contributions by managing their effective tax rates, many do not typically pursue, nor do they provide incentives for their tax executives to pursue, the significant cash-flow benefits the tax function can often generate.

In many instances, negative economic positions can be tempered with proactive tax planning that can lead to immediate cash flow.

A market contraction provides further opportunities to energize tax departments: taken together, income, property, franchise, and other taxes can often be one of the largest costs incurred in corporate America. In many instances, negative economic positions can be tempered with proactive tax planning that can lead to immediate cash flow.

Some companies may also be experiencing a tightening risk market, whether from property and business insurers looking for ways to limit payouts and lessen liability or from health insurance providers seeking to raise premiums. In light of these developments, companies may need to reexamine their insurance plans. If so, it's smart to involve your tax departments. They can examine the propriety of creating or maintaining a self-insurance arrangement and can be instrumental in making current arrangements more tax-efficient by accelerating deductions, reducing expenses, and properly managing reserves.

In these ways, tax departments can perform double duty. Not only can they be employed to keep an eye on lowering the company's effective income tax rate, but, equally important in a downturn, they can also become actively involved in developing strategies that can yield immediate cash-flow benefits. A key starting point, according to KPMG tax partner, Dale Currie, is inventorying your tax attributes. "Many times the focus is on one transaction when they really should be looking at several to see where they can do pairing of attributes for optimal benefit," he explained.

CREATING A CASH CUSHION

If reducing friction, strictures, and curbs on momentum is one of the fundamental pillars of business agility, then cash is central. One of the concerns economists express about the ability of global economies to spring back from contraction is the underlying ill health of corporate financial structures. Looking at the most recent contraction in the United States, one can see that what has happened to consumer America is reflected in many respects by corporate America, specifically, record high debt burdens and poor liquidity. In a word, we are over-extended.

The communications industry is feeling this especially heavily. According to the debt rating company, Fitch IBCA, Duff & Phelps, the first half of 2001 saw $13.9 billion of telecommunications bonds default, with investor losses of $12.8 billion. This is over two times the amount of similar losses suffered in all of 2000. *Business Week* calls free operating cash flow the communications industry's "holy grail" metric, but the ramp-up in bandwidth over the last several years has saddled some communications companies with so much debt that it could be a couple of years before they see any free cash flow. In Europe, the problem is exacerbated by the enormously high prices, in some cases in excess of $200 billion, that many European telecommunications companies had to pay their governments for the license rights to provide advanced wireless offerings. Many are attempting to renegotiate more favorable and lower terms, but in the meanwhile the license costs are a bitter pill to swallow in what is already a painful industry slump.

The communications industry is hardly alone. Debt runs high on many corporate books. The focus now is restructuring it. Exposed creditors may well be inclined to extend more favorable terms, such as delayed payments, short-term adjusted rates, and even additional financing as a way of also protecting their own interests. Some indebted firms will seek partners or investors to provide needed liquidity in exchange for a piece of the business. Still others will look to divest non-core businesses or assets. The tradeoffs may be less than ideal,

The tradeoffs may be less than ideal, but if the business has strong prospects and needs some oxygen to get it to the next peak, they may be worth it.

but if the business has strong prospects and needs some oxygen to get it to the next peak, they may be worth it.

If market contractions serve to ground us back into a profitability mindset, expansions can distract focus from the need to be continually focused on cash generation. As Stuart Campbell, chief financial officer of RightChoice Managed Care, Inc., pointed out in an article for the *St. Louis Business*

Journal, investors and analysts often focus on companies' earnings, but profits aren't everything. "Cash is king. If people are truly generating cash equal to or in excess of earnings you can bet it's a solid company."

Emerson, the Missouri-based electronics company, gets high marks for its longstanding tradition of management excellence. The company has been one of the most consistent performers in the *Fortune* 500 with over 44 quarters of consecutive growth. One of the reasons is CEO David Farr's zealous focus on cash. In addition to aggressively monitoring capital spending costs, Farr ties incentive compensation to management's success in expediting cash collection on accounts. Managers across every division are required to spend one full day a month developing very detailed monthly reports. As Farr noted in a *Harvard Business Review* piece, "Moving Upward in a Downturn," "Everyone who provides input to a division head spends one day per month focused on the future of the business. So if anyone sees a weakness, a plan to deal with it is immediately created." This is one reason why the business posts among the best free cash flow-per-share ratios among companies in its industry.

By focusing on cash, companies like Emerson acquire a tremendous amount of flexibility and freedom, in terms of strong credit ratings, favorable borrowing terms, and increased buying muscle for acquisitions. Compare this with a debt-strapped competitor whose interest commitments require a more risk-averse, cautious stance, and it is easy to see which company is best positioned to exploit a market recovery. That is business agility.

CONCLUSION

The experiences of agile companies that have made cost management part of their operating cultures suggest that a practice of rewarding innovation in cost reduction pays powerful dividends in uncertain business environments. While individual approaches to running a lean operation vary, two consistent themes emerge—the benefits of encouraging managers to identify and "own" imaginative changes in the way they do business and an emphasis on strategic and targeted cost reduction that recognizes differences in individual business priorities. The following represent some of those collected best practices.

The Agile Business Approach to Cost Management

❏ Project forward to what the business will need on the upside of the economic cycle. Cut strategically with an eye to the long term, rather than mandating reductions that will just require replacements in kind as business strengthens.

❏ Proactively manage the cost reduction process so that it is consistent with strategic business priorities. Focus on aligning and defining targeted cost improvement opportunities with individual business requirements instead of establishing "across the board" goals.

❏ Identify changes in one's organizational structure and processes that can create long-term efficiencies and productivity improvements rather than simply cutting headcount. Oftentimes significant changes in the way a business operates can reduce costs while at the same time providing revenue upside through greater customer focus or other market-facing benefits.

❑ Analyze aggregated costs by category across the company. It is not uncommon to find small cost categories in individual business units that represent significant spending for the corporation as a whole. Many of these (like travel, advertising, marketing services, supplies, etc.) can be purchased and managed centrally with large cost savings due to greater purchasing scale and leverage.

❑ Consider creative approaches to addressing high-cost fixed expenses like real estate and equipment. Encouraging telecommuting, for example, reduces the cost of the physical plant while, at the same time, yielding substantial benefits in productivity and staff morale.

❑ Explore cost reduction opportunities derived from proactive financial management and other "intangi bles." Opportunities abound in tax planning, effective cash and receivables management, debt restructuring, and credit terms.

❑ Collectively, agile companies tell us that they can stay lean while still capitalizing on opportunities by approaching cost management flexibly and creatively.

CHAPTER NINE

Polishing the Stone

In far-flung places of the world are generations of families whose art is handling rough-hewn topaz and emeralds and rubies. By holding them to the light carefully, examining their intrinsic characteristics painstakingly, and smoothing and polishing them meticulously, they allow the stone's strongest qualities to emerge to best advantage. Contrast that with one of the favorite pastimes of a child in summer, that of going out into one's backyard, finding a few neat rocks, and slamming them against each other to see what interesting things might be seen inside. A similar paradigm may be said to exist in some corporate structures with respect to the continual and effective management of costs.

Cutting costs and planning for growth can be cyclical activities. When the outlook is grim, we rein in. When it opens up, we do, too. Agility is enhanced by twinning the two activities and making them a constant way of managing the business. "You should always be looking at cutting cost and being efficient even when times are good," said Ed Breen formerly of Motoroal. But all too often, a corporate overhaul is made when one's back is against the wall. Instead, detailed process review should be an ongoing, enterprise-wide activity. In the words of Tom Ryder, profiled below, "reengineering is constant."

A READER'S DIGEST STORY

Tom Ryder became the head of *Reader's Digest* in 1998. At the time, growth, profits, and share prices were unimpressive. Within a year, though, Ryder managed to reverse the situation. Since then, corporate earnings have more than doubled, two major acquisitions have been made, and the company is being recapitalized to replace the majority block of voting shares owned by two charities. We talked with Ryder to explore both the set of issues he faced when he first took over the top seat and his approach to resolving them.

The company Ryder inherited was reeling from three years of steep revenue declines. "The *Digest*," he said, "had been pilloried in the press. Management was demoralized and investors were readying for revolution." It was, he said wryly, "a cheery situation." But, as Ryder told us, "Faced with no possibilities, you can achieve truly remarkable results."

In attempting to staunch the flow, Ryder saw that his first task was to define reality, stark though it might have been. He started by holding a company-wide meeting with his entire staff, broadcasting the proceedings by satellite to far-flung locations and with videos to those spots unreachable by satellite. (The *Digest* is a truly global operation.) In it, he made some powerful statements about what had to be done. "Yes," he said, "things were difficult. But this is a fabulous franchise with fabulous assets and, though the immediate past has been bleak, the future doesn't have to be, and that future starts with us." When asked if there were going to be layoffs, Ryder stated simply and directly that "yes, there would be."

Next, he started looking for places to cut cost. When the board was interviewing him for the position, they explained that all the cuts that could be made had been made. There was nothing left to trim. But Ryder had come to *Reader's Digest* from American Express and had "spent every day of the last 15 years reengineering companies." What he saw was that prior cost reductions were of a type that said, "Take 10% out of the budget" and "silly things" like "tell people to take time off."

Ryder brought in an outside group and set some crisp targets, which he announced quickly to executives. He admits that the targets, which were pretty tough, seemed laughable at the time. They were, he said, "conceived by me with a little bit of experience, a little bit of knowledge, and a lot of hope." We should state up front, that Ryder is a pretty humble guy.

The target he set was that within three years, they would reduce their cost base by $300 million and improve profitability by $100 million. The process by which this was all to be done sounds a bit glib, he said, but had three steps, "stop stupid stuff." The notion was "let's get together and be sensible. Where we're spending foolishly, let's stop." Areas that fell into the category of "stupid" included a fairly massive underwriting of cafeteria expenses, bus service from the train to the office, overspending on certain promotional efforts, and the elimination of art tours and an entire curatorial staff who oversaw the art collection acquired under the Wallaces, the founders of *Reader's Digest*.

Interestingly, Ryder assigned responsibility for identifying the list of cuts, not to top corporate brass, but to the individual process owners. He figured that they knew far better than he where the fat was. And it appeared they did. In two years (one year shy of the goal) the company took out $405 million in cost, $105 million more than was set as the target. Within the same period, the company also achieved a profit of $200 million, double the original $100 million goal.

> Interestingly, Ryder assigned responsibility for identifying the list of cuts, not to top corporate brass, but to the individual process owners.

Aside from the obvious empowerment that employees derived from participating directly in the restructuring process, Ryder believed it helped to instill an important cost-cutting discipline. To make it work, recognizing that cutting is a whole lot less fun than building, Ryder helped motivate his team by tying executive compensation to the transformation goals.

He recognized that he had to restore investor confidence in his company's ability to generate regular earnings and reinvest its capital back into the business. To accomplish this, Ryder knew that a critical parallel strategy was needed, and that was a plan for growth. So he established a separate and concurrent growth track than would run independently of his ongoing reengineering work.

Ryder's growth initiative involves acquiring two, three, or four foundation stone properties, new businesses that would stand alone but get core business support. It is an approach that leverages his brand and, as Ryder says, "allows us to grow in certain important ways." To date, he has acquired three new properties—Books Are Fun, World's Finest Chocolate (which was merged into QSP), and Reiman Publications. Together these businesses bring in $1 billion in revenue and $150 million in profit. If he can acquire two more, Ryder says that he will have created a series of businesses growing at 15% a year that together will equal the size of the core business five years ago. If the new business continues to be as successful as it is now, Ryder says, "we'll use it as a lever to restore our core business."

Ryder's experience shows that continual refinement is something he and his team take seriously. And the benefits speak for themselves. Above all else, what the *Reader's Digest* story teaches us is that one must cut and sow at the same time. Agile companies make constant attention to cost management and revenue growth their twin embedded disciplines. It is a process that starts with establishing the right mindset.

ESTABLISHING THE RIGHT MINDSET— CONTINUAL REFINEMENT

Continual refinement as a practice and pursuit has existed in varying degrees and with varying success for decades. First demonstrated by the indomitable Frederic Taylor and his spirited time and motion studies of Pennsylvania steelworkers, the practice of continual refinement has acquired different names and emphasis since its start in the late 1800s. In more recent times, these paths have coalesced giving rise in the early 1990s to a more formal movement with mass appeal, known as reengineering.

As first conceived, reengineering was intended to help companies undergo a one-time, rapid process redesign. Old processes were swapped for newly designed, market-facing practices that were aimed at lowering cycle time, improving product and service quality, reducing process costs, and enhancing revenue opportunities.

But with the surging economy of the mid-90s, companies began to diverge from their original efficiency and cost-cutting focus. Enticed by the burgeoning opportunities engendered by new digital technologies and the Internet economy, corporate focus increasingly shifted toward strategies aimed at growth, and the more "humdrum" reengineering task of core process refinement fell into neglect.

The decline of reengineering was exacerbated by the overemphasis many early programs placed on tactical changes and the less than optimal results these changes generated. Compared with the level of organizational "pain" generated by the process review, the benefits seemed in question. And so, for most, the concept degenerated from a hot, must-have business practice into something seen as just one more consulting sales push.

But even during the height of the "roaring 90s," some agile executives continued to nurture the concept of reengineering,

**The decline of reengi-
neering was exacerbated
by the overemphasis
many early programs
placed on tactical
changes and the less
than optimal results
these changes generated.**

evolving the practice into what one dubbed "continual tinkering." In so doing, they have elevated the approach from the tactical to the strategic and have made the following three elements the heart of their strategic refinement program.

Agile businesses ground their strategic refinement program on these three areas:

❏ Constant adaptation
❏ Establishing a flexible cost structure
❏ Planning for revenue growth at all times

Agile business leaders create a culture of looking *internally* as well as externally for value and growth opportunities, and of communicating *internally* as well as externally with key constituents to measure and assess market demands. By so "living in their markets," to quote McGraw of McGraw-Hill, agile executives have become more sophisticated in their objective, that of continually aligning core processes to the demands and possibilities of the market.

CONSTANT ADAPTATION

Agile businesses constantly adapt to avoid obsolescence. While the recent bubble brought its share of hype, it is important that executives not let that shroud the real benefits of digital transformation. Obsolescence is a pervasive business risk.

Digital technologies, if allied to pressing business issues and not acquired simply for the sake of the technology, are there to help companies become more responsive to their customers, achieve real productivity gains, and enhance profitability. Together they work to keep obsolescence at bay.

The Harry Fox Agency (HFA) was established in 1927. It is the largest music licensing and royalty collection agency in the world. During the last decade, the agency saw its overwhelming market share advantage shrink and its revenue base begin to erode. This occurred as other music industry participants used emerging technologies such as the Web to sidestep traditional licensing intermediaries like HFA. It was a classic case of the phenomenon Harvard Business School professor, Clayton Christiansen, termed in his book, *The Innovator's Dilemma*, "disruptive technology."

History is replete with examples of well-managed companies failing to sustain themselves as their industries were transformed by new technologies. None of the makers of 8-inch hard disk drives were able to lead the industry move to the smaller floppy size. Some of the old discount department stores such as Sears and Montgomery Ward struggled in the advent of cheaper big-box stores. Charles Schwab's innovative move into electronic trading and discount brokerage once threatened the traditional brokerage firm model. In this same way, the World Wide Web was beginning to threaten HFA's standard means of doing business. Left unheeded, such disruptive technologies can eventually lead to complete obsolescence if the older, mainstream company proves unable to adapt its business to the new model.

But this was not going to happen to Harry Fox. The agency determined that it was not about to be mainstreamed. HFA sought to prevent further declines by transforming its business processes in two ways. The first task was to migrate its old manual licensing processes to ones that were Web-based and supported with fully automated back-office processing. The second thing it did was focus on developing a more aggressive, entrepreneurial culture, one that emphasized proactive business development and customer service. Through this joint approach, HFA offered its clients three important improvements: shortened licensing times, improved customer service, and very advanced information databases. Judging by a spate of recent announcements, the agency's emphasis on adaptation has served it well. It has launched an Internet subscription service and can now issue licenses for hundreds of thousands of musical works for delivery over the Internet.

Agile companies understand the business imperative to constantly adapt to avoid being a victim of disruptive technologies and the risk of obsolescence and irrelevance. This is why those companies that continually refine their processes are those whose market face will be the most relevant and responsive. This will not happen if strategic process review occurs only during the soul-searching periods of economic contraction. Instead, the fruits will go to those that make it an ongoing discipline.

> **This is why those companies that continually refine their processes are those whose market face will be the most relevant and responsive.**

Be Decisive

In an earlier chapter, we stressed the importance of deliberation in thinking and planning, this as a counterpoint to many
of the hasty, impatient practices of the past several years. Here
we stress that in concert with the need to be deliberate is the
need to be purposeful.

Indecision can take many forms, most of them unhelpful.
Some businesses may be indecisive about their purpose. Is it
strategic or financial? What's more important, shipping the
first product or bringing in the most revenue? Depending on
the answer—product, revenue, or both—a company will act
and invest in different ways. But for many companies, the
particular strategic direction may not be very clear and that
can hamper a company's ability to take swift action.

Other companies are indecisive structurally. Businesses
that yo-yo in their commitment to certain initiatives or
departments—for example, funding marketing and customer
service heavily one year, then cutting back sharply the next—
are not uncommon. This can happen frequently with leadership changes. People advance and their replacements bring
different operating philosophies and goals. The new ideas can
be great, but flip-flopping financing, strategy, and messaging
create instability and waste. Agile businesses gain better trac-
tion during transition when reasonable continuity is maintained in core processes and functions.

Similar equivocation has hampered many joint ventures.
Many companies that loudly championed their support of
key joint ventures quietly developed competing products

within their own shop. This was done just in case ... just in case the venture failed or its "trusted" partners were doing the same. Ironically, such mixed backing has emerged as the single most common reason for the failure of joint ventures to achieve promised goals.

Indecision necessarily comes from uncertainty. We know that it is essential for agile companies to focus tightly on their core businesses and strategies, but this can be difficult for companies that aren't confident of their ability to pick the right strategy. In the absence of surety, logic says hedge your bets. Witness the millions invested by companies on myriad e-business initiatives during the period of e-mania. No one knew exactly how the New Economy would unfold, so parallel investments seemed a sound approach.

The problem, according to a report by Mercer Management Consulting, is that many of these initiatives are "still alive and kicking and requesting more capital." Often externally focused in the extreme, these initiatives were frequently divorced from the company's actual business imperatives. In total, according to the Mercer study, "they probably represented more wasted investment than the far more visible dot.com fiasco."

Agile business leaders have the courage to be decisive. When Motorola acquired General Instrument, Motorola's CEO, Chris Galvin, challenged Ed Breen, then executive vice president, to integrate staff and products and develop the combined entity's strategic plan. Where so many business combinations go awry, Breen's integration was accomplished swiftly and successfully. When asked what contributed to his success, Breen indicated that decisiveness was a key criterion.

"It's much better to take action quickly," he states. People get jittery when there's a merger, reorganization, or other major structural change. "Once the plan is set," Breen stresses, "you need to be decisive and get it out of the way. That way you can free the organization to focus on the core goal. To get 'one plus one to equal three,' you move thoughtfully, but act

> **"To get 'one plus one to equal three,' you move thoughtfully, but act decisively."**
>
> **—Ed Breen, former President and COO, Motorola**

decisively." We focus on this point because the ability of a company to permeate clear, articulated decisions throughout its enterprise directly influences that company's ability to execute. And in fragile competitive or economic environments, execution is paramount.

ESTABLISHING A FLEXIBLE COST STRUCTURE

We have discussed how important it is for agile businesses to continually adapt and refine. Having such a culture embedded will help companies take the next step, that of maintaining a flexible cost structure. When we say "flexible cost structure," we're not talking about fixed or variable costs and adjusting the balance between them. Instead, we are talking about an employee-"owned" approach that continually assesses the value and efficacy of current processes, compares alternative ways of achieving the process goal, and creates leverage and scale where possible. The advantages of a flexible cost structure are that it makes a company alert to change, vigorous in responding, lean in approach, but strong in executing a course of action.

Creating Efficiency—Streamlining and Standardizing

Designing flexibility into one's cost structure is very difficult to do. Frequently contributing to the difficulty is the manner in which financial information is generated and collected. Without a consistent enterprise-wide revenue and cost reporting system that managers in the field and at headquarters can feed into and "hear back" from, ad hoc collection systems inevitably grow to fill the void. Business unit heads can churn out cost reports every week, but if each is using different formats and different criteria, it would take someone with seer-like vision to identify trouble spots, track costs, and make projections.

When Tom Glocer took over as CEO of the venerable news and information organization, Reuters, he observed that the proud 150-year-old company operated more like a federation of local and regional businesses than it did a streamlined international corporation. He noted that every country manager ran its own separate business, managed its own news operation, and prepared its own profit and loss statement. This localized ownership helped ensure Reuters' responsiveness in reacting to news events, but it created problems from a financial management perspective. One of these was that, under the current structure, country managers did not provide a budget for major unplanned events. As theirs was a news business, unplanned events happened with some frequency. This in turn subjected budgets to frequent hits.

To design more flexibility and control into the system, Glocer created a single consolidated budget for editorial under which he rolled all of the local and regional news budgets. Consolidating the budget clearly made it much easier to manage effectively the whole business. It also made it considerably easier for Glocer to assess variances and plan for contingencies. Observing that "it's a bit like risk sharing in the insurance industry," Glocer now provides enough additional monies on a macro level to cover major crises. In addition, the discipline provided by Glocer's consolidated editorial budget process greatly facilitates his management's ability to be responsive to business changes in moving and accounting for funds. That, of course, is what agility is all about.

Standardizing core processes, such as financial reporting, grants managers increased operating flexibility because it gives them:

❑ Knowledge across their enterprise,
❑ Control across their enterprise,
❑ An ability to model and test across their enterprise, and
❑ An ability to execute changes swiftly across their enterprise.

Selective Versus Wholesale Change

But there is also a danger in placing too heavy an emphasis on process. It is for this that bureaucracies the world over are maligned, for their tenacious over-adherence to process for process's sake. Far less extreme but far more pervasive is the ebb and flow of corporate philosophy over whether it is best to centralize or decentralize. The issue here is not the approach. Proponents of either cause can make a good case. Rather, it is the tendency for management to adopt whichever chosen path in toto. And this can be a problem because agility is as much dependent on discernment as on streamlined automation.

The more robust mindset is one that keeps the desired business objectives uppermost, whether that be a defined focus on core products, core markets, core customers, or some combination thereof. The companies then tightly align the necessary structure and processes in support of those objectives. What most agile companies find is that, depending on their strategic goals, their business, and their industry, they will seek to centralize and automate certain processes and decentralize others.

> **What most agile companies find is that, depending on their strategic goals, their business, and their industry, they will seek to centralize and automate certain processes and decentralize others.**

In general, agile businesses derive greater cost flexibility by:

❑ Centralizing and/or automating low-judgment, low-value, and low-customization tasks

❑ Decentralizing high-judgment, high-value, and high-customization tasks

❏ Standardizing cost and productivity improvements and ensuring consistency across the enterprise.

An example of this approach is the tack taken by Avaya. When Avaya was spun out of Lucent in October 2000, Garry McGuire was installed as the CFO. A veteran of many reorganizations, McGuire found that experience valuable in shepherding the new organization toward its joint objectives of restructuring the business (developing a flexible cost structure) and reinvesting in new product areas (planning for growth). One of the nice things he found about starting from scratch was that "as a new company we could design our cost structure." In starting with a blank slate, McGuire could engage teams of people at the process level and identify process improvement opportunities. His teams found a number of ready opportunities in short order. In addressing them, McGuire insisted that all process improvements be standardized so that "any cost improvements could be sustainable even in the ramp-up period."

> One of the nice things he found about starting from scratch was that "as a new company we could design our cost structure."

But though he desired the efficiencies that came with consistency, McGuire was keen to emphasize the need for his managers to be thoughtful about what it was they standardized. "There's no question," he said, "that you need to have discipline to deliver lower costs to the customer. But it is also critical to balance creativity against controls and process. You need to free your people to be creative and focus on the high-value activities." To obtain that balance, McGuire says, "Focus on the low value-add things and standardize and systematize the process."

In lieu of broad-brush standardization techniques, McGuire recognizes that, while deliberation is a virtue, prompt action is a necessity. "Certainly management needs to be careful not to 'kill the business' while taking things out," McGuire admits. "But," he cautions, "you must also recognize that the human tendency is 'let's get ready to act.'" In the process, he adds, "Don't be afraid to break things." Rather than trying to avoid breakages, plan for them and thus be prepared to "fix the holes that arise."

Scale and Leverage—Shared Services and Outsourcing

Recognizing that the shelf life of any organization design is probably less than a year, agile leaders focus on the manner in which all business processes work together to support the corporate strategy, rather than simply refining specific processes for efficiency alone. The goal is strategic scale and leverage. To achieve it, one first needs to assess the current process costs and eliminate duplication. Gather data on all of the categories of cost related to a given key process or function. Observe how widely or narrowly those costs are dispersed around the enterprise. Then corral them in the manner that best fits your business. For instance, after one company completed its internal process review, it discovered that 52% of its data processing activities occurred outside the area indicated for that function on the company's organization chart.

For optimal scale and leverage, some businesses create shared services centers. A shared services center groups together key assets and resources to serve the strategic aims of the company's business units. This type of approach can be a powerful method to enhance the value of internal support functions. In contrast to centralization, which can be too process-laden, and decentralization, which can be too costly, shared services centers can provide a more sophisticated medium for managing key functions. The distinction lies in its ethos. Rather than mandating control of the business, the shared services center operates at its behest. Thus, the structure exists to support the goals, not the other way around.

In keeping with the more strategic filament underlying shared service centers, the entire value chain is included. The spectrum of shared services center opportunities can consist of:

❑ **Sales and customer service:** order processing, telemarketing, account management, claims processing and support

❑ **Finance:** accounts payable, accounts receivable, travel, treasury, and general accounting

❑ **Information technology:** network and desktop support, Web site management, data center operations, enterprise project management, and telecommunications

❑ **Human resources:** payroll, benefits, retirement, training, and recruitment

❑ **Infrastructure:** purchasing, logistics, construction, and real estate services

Many of the executives we spoke with for this book point to shared services centers as an important resource for building agility and flexibility into their cost structure. For Glocer of Reuters, they are "a best practice." At Reuters, Glocer says, "We use shared services centers to run help desks in every country." Focused on the goal of keeping customer satisfaction rates high, Glocer has equipped his centers with intelligent telephony and customer relationship management systems. "Quite simply," he says, "they offer lower cost, higher performance, and better customer service 24/7."

> **Many of the executives we spoke with for this book point to shared services centers as an important resource for building agility and flexibility into their cost structure.**

In building a customer contact center for a promising startup, Avaya designed a way to help the company from both financial and customer service standpoints.

For the former, Avaya made the call center virtual. Some of the company's call center attendees are work-at-home mothers. Now, their call center is the kitchen table. By making the call center virtual, the young company's army of work-at-home moms acquired time and schedule flexibility and the business eliminated expensive physical plant overhead costs.

To enhance customer service, Avaya equipped the call center with intelligent routing technology that directed its client's premium customers to the proper customer contact person. "We manage the intelligent routing of their customer

calls," says McGuire, "so the higher-revenue-potential customers go to the front of the queue and are directed to the
higher-performing attendants, those that have a track record
of raising the total customer order size." As a result of both
efforts, the startup has seen its costs come down and its customer service record rise.

Outsourcing and Focusing on the Core Business

An alternative approach to shared services is outsourcing. It
can be difficult to look objectively at elements of the business
into which a lot of blood, sweat, and tears have been poured,
particularly if your company has been involved in those areas
for years. But agile businesses learn not to be sentimental
about any part of their business.

Ryder experienced this firsthand at *Reader's Digest*.
Fulfillment was a huge part of the company's traditional business. The problem, as Ryder discovered, was that it didn't
relate to the core. Ryder's core business, he says, "is to create
products, market them, and manage suppliers." He adds, "If
we are going to perform other services outside of these areas,
we must meet the test of doing them faster, better, or cheaper
than anyone else." With this focus now uppermost, *Reader's
Digest* outsources its fulfillment practice along with a host of
other services.

Outsourcing can also be useful for companies that are
going through the process of fine-tuning what they feel their
core go-to-market offering should be. Sometimes it can help
just clear away some of the noise.

For example, when Carl Vogel was named CEO of Charter Communications in the thick of the 2001 downturn, he realized right away that in a turbulent market it was more important than ever to focus on what you can do well and let others do the rest. In assessing Charter, Vogel saw that "they probably had too many people and a fair amount of waste." To get better clarity, he decided to "outsource the delta until we have a good sense of what we have." Outsourcing serves a tremendously valuable role he feels because "you don't have to have all your people doing all of your stuff."

Flexibility and Continual Refinement

Building flexibility into one's cost structure is a continual process. To make it work, agile businesses engage people at the process level to identify improvements. They give employees ownership for developing recommendations and implementing cost and productivity improvements. They align the company's reward systems to make sure that they are in support of the process. In this way, agile businesses provide employees with a vested interest and let them put some "skin" in the game. Motivation and incentive are the root of all sustainable action.

It is easy to overlook internal policies, but these often bear scrutiny as well. For example, some organizations may be staffed based on a policy or strategy that drives how many people are needed. Where that is the case, it is better to determine if such numbers reflect the current operating environment.

When mandating or implementing changes, be sure to factor in enough time for process changes to take effect. Work does tend to expand to fill all available time, so it is important to be aggressive. But be too aggressive and employees lose heart and management risks losing credibility. Be realistic and honest. Finally, communicate your plan and its intended goals so that expectations are managed, directions are clear, and the improvements that are made are made well.

Thus far, in describing the practice of continual refinement, we have discussed:

❏ The need to constantly adapt—in order *to stay alert* to opportunity;
❏ The need to build flexibility and consistency into one's cost structure—in order *to prepare* the company *to act* on opportunity;

Now we present the third element,

❏ The need to plan for revenue growth at all times—in order *to focus and execute* on carefully selected opportunities.

PLANNING FOR REVENUE GROWTH AT ALL TIMES

As stated at the outset of this chapter, people tend to plan for growth when the economy is faring well, and people tend to retrench when the tide goes the other way. On the face of it, the instinct appears sensible. When the economy is robust, the risk window is open much wider and the penalties of an error in judgment are less severe. Investors, analysts, and other constituents are more inclined to give you the benefit of the doubt. Market psychology is positive and that works in your favor. But during a contraction, a recession or an industry slump, these same factors reverse themselves, making it both realistically and psychologically harder to plan for a rebound that is as yet invisible.

Nonetheless, agility is best established by those companies that continuously plan for growth regardless of economic season. The reason for this is threefold: time to market, competitive sustainability, and consistency.

Those companies that wait for the signs of economic rebirth to become tangible, risk significant exposure.

Revenue growth can come from various sources—organically through new product development, or an uptick in orders for current products, or artificially through an acquisition, merger, or joint venture, to name but a few. However, the reality is that while the avenues may be plentiful, most take a considerable amount of time to nurture. It is rare, for example, for a product to be conceived, created, and launched in anything under eight months, and that's pushing things. Most deals take even longer to vet, close, and integrate. Those companies that wait for the signs of economic rebirth to become tangible, risk significant exposure.

Competitors that have taken advantage of the downturn's lull to mature select innovations, improve inventories, exploit cross-marketing opportunities, refine branding and messaging, and bolster their pool of "best and brightest" are those who have put themselves in the best position for action the minute new orders start to percolate onto the books once again. All others are left to catch up. That is the reality. Sustainability depends on a steady and consistent approach to growth planning.

For those that feel they can "make up for it" when the market improves, there is the additional danger of turning the spending spigot on too quickly. The herky-jerky inconsistency of deep cuts during the throes of contraction followed by heavy spending to repair the cuts in the rebound, damages morale and productivity and, worse, often places that company in a position of repeating the pattern when the economic cycle next trails down. Spending alone does not beget revenue. The relationship between the two is indirect. So, if spending is the only card one holds when the chairman of the Federal Reserve presents his cryptically optimistic picture of the economy, one must hold one's breath that the card will be enough to trump the other risks. And that is an avoidable position.

The better approach is one that makes a point of always planning for growth. "What you try to do is develop a habit," says Morgan. "You shrink travel and inventories and population, but you can't spend too long doing that. You have to get everybody focused on things that will position you better for coming out the other side. And you have to get people into that mode quickly."

In order to focus his people well, Morgan understands that management needs to know what's coming down the line and that means keeping one eye constantly trained on the horizon. "People don't anticipate what's next," he states. "But anticipating the next step is really what the senior people get paid for." At Applied Materials, Morgan's board meetings deliberately eliminate operational review from the discussion. "We do a three-slide summary," he states. "The rest is about things we're looking at for our future. The other stuff—numbers, headcount, margins, inventory, turns, cash—that's all in the operations book, which is sent out two weeks prior to the meeting."

> **It takes as much discipline to remain attentive to signs of trouble as it does to signs of hope.**

Anticipation and planning are intrinsic to agility. Together they reduce surprises and help executives manage for consistency. It takes as much discipline to remain attentive to signs of trouble as it does to signs of hope, but those who embrace that discipline will be rewarded with considerably more operating freedom.

Grow, but Grow from Your Core

Most executives are not deluded about the wisdom of concentrating their best resources and efforts on those activities allied to their business's intrinsic strengths. They understand that it is prudent to attend to those activities that will burnish and exploit those strengths and extend them into new markets. But these same leaders understand that business is not static. Opportunities abound and competitive pressure compels them to act quickly and act often.

Management consultants espouse the cardinal rule that expansion makes sense only if it directly benefits the core business. This advice is eminently logical, particularly during times of contraction, but pity the executive during our recent e-mania faced with staring down a roomful of impatient investors and explaining that they would not be embarking on an e-strategy because the current benefits did not support the core business.

In general, companies should avoid entering markets where they have limited experience. A good rule of thumb is to exploit new ventures only on the back of experience and invest only where the expertise is proven. When economic conditions are favorable, carefully managed diversification can make sense, but most strategists suggest avoiding this during a contraction. The theoretical benefits of limited exposure from a more varied market base can often be erased by the dilution of resources and management attention on the main business.

This does not mean that companies stop acquiring or investing. As noted in our chapter on contrarianism, a contraction offers agile businesses fantastic opportunities to buy assets that add to their core strengths, at modest prices. Likewise, strategic investments in select and important research and development initiatives are also vital to sustained growth. In an environment where others are cutting back, a market contraction is precisely the time to focus talent on enhancing the business. As Darrell Rigby noted in *Harvard Business Review*, "The surprising insight is that—assuming the core business is worth holding and growing— focused acquisitions (and R&D investment) should reduce risk, not increase it."

Innovation and Synergy

In addition to select, focused investments, agile businesses also aggressively seek intelligent synergies and cross-marketing opportunities. Look for opportunities to diffuse investments over multiple product lines and channels. The media industry has made doing so a specialty. Companies like AOL/TimeWarner cross-market products widely. New films are promoted in print, on television, and in online ads, on Web sites, and in chat groups. Product extensions are developed as "accessories" and merchandized separately across their portfolio of businesses for additional, linked revenue streams.

Similar strategies can be pursued in other industries. Whether your business is in electronics, communications, software, or services, "the marketplace," says Avaya's McGuire, "is looking at solutions not discrete products. Thus," he says, "our perspective must also be looking along industry lines and solutions."

When agile businesses examine new product initiatives, they look for extension and penetration potential. We live in a disposable society. Many companies, like many households, fall victim to tossing out what might be recycled, repurposed, sold outright, or donated for tax purposes(!). Return on investment depends partly on how well one milks the investment. This is where structure can be used to support strategy. Agile businesses keep the research and development door open to other voices and other departments. They add the word "adapt" to the standard build-or-buy analysis. They winnow the number of competing internal initiatives and ensure that the top two, three, five are seeded and fertilized across the entire horizontal organization.

Agile businesses bring the same scrutiny to external opportunities. Rather than branching into new sectors during a market contraction, savvy businesses look for holes in their current field of battle. They ask questions: Where are my competitors pulling back? Where are their customers being underserved or overcharged? How can I exploit those gaps?

This is precisely what JetBlue Airways did during the airline industry implosion in fall 2001. The company's strategic planners scanned their computerized reservation system to pick out areas where other airlines had cut back on their schedules. As *Fast Company* (December 2001) reported, "They zeroed in on Florida, where American Airlines, Delta Express, US Airways, and MetroJet had all recently slashed their schedules. ... Less than two months after the tragedy, JetBlue inaugurated seven new flights to Florida, boosting service by 44%." JetBlue used tactics available to all companies in every industry to turn an "unsung" opportunity into a strategy for revenue growth. They observed, they got the facts, and they executed. Sometimes, it is that simple.

Finally, we recall the truth in Carl Vogel's assertion, "If a customer can't see the difference, then you don't need to spend the money." In planning for growth, agile businesses remain mindful of the customer experience. They make sure customers are aware and that they care. Otherwise, the corollary of Vogel's assertion suggests, "If customers can't see the difference, they won't spend the money."

CONCLUSION—CONFIDENCE, COHESION, AND A SENSE OF PURPOSE

Vodafone's CEO, Christopher Gent, said, "Internal cohesion and a sense of purpose are what power the engine of growth." He summed it up perfectly. By continually refining one's business practices with an eye toward growth in good times and in bad, a company becomes better able to weather all economic seasons while moving powerfully ahead with the core business strategy. It's a matter of believing in oneself. While riding the roller coaster of a cyclical business might make others reach for the package of antacids, we are struck by Morgan's quiet confidence. He simply takes the view that it is better for people in his company to make up their minds that they are in a great business and have hope for the long term. Quiet belief, strong discipline—for agile businesses, there is no other choice.

> **Internal cohesion and a sense of purpose are what power the engine of growth.**
> **Christopher Gent,**
> **CEO, Vodafone**

CHAPTER TEN

The Search for Value

From vision to viability to value: that is our natural progression in testing an idea. What can we be? How can we be? What does it mean to be?

In this chapter, we explore the search for value. How do we shape our business models to optimize value? How do we examine existing assets to measure value? How do we improve reporting to make that value more transparent?

CHANGING VALUE MODELS

A few years back, all it took to kick-start animated discussion amongst a group of businesspeople was to casually blurt the question, "What do you think is king?" This would generally set off a raging debate on the checkerboard of the new economy. There were those who would make *channel* king and others who felt *content* deserved the role. The new economy undulated and people made their bets.

But now, in these more reflective times, there are those who feel that the wizard has been unveiled and that the customer has been behind the lever the whole time. This was certainly the sentiment at the most recent convocation of the World Economic Forum in New York City. The annual gathering, which attracts corporate, government, and academic leaders from around the world, serves as a yearly barometer of executive opinion. For that reason, it is interesting to note that one of the strong messages to emerge is that we have moved from a content-centric to a customer-centric world wherein those companies that are closest to the customer will win in the digital age. Steve Case, chairman of AOL Time Warner, echoed the thoughts of many at the gathering when he said that "the role [of companies] will be to empower consumers to be in control of their information, communication, entertainment, and education."

Of course, the notion of the customer being king is not staggeringly new. Remember those department store signs of old exhorting staff to be mindful that "the customer is always right." The customer has always been important. But digital transformation has narrowed the distance between businesses and their customers. The same evolution has given customers a much louder voice when it comes to influencing business strategy and output.

The thinking seems to be that those distributors that succeed in becoming the "infomediary" in physical delivery and customer care will be successful in the digital age. Therefore, customer billing, customer care, simple integration, and personalization will be keys to success in the digital world. As one Australian business publication put it, "Demand from customers is driving the change process. They are telling us they want one bill and one call center. It is convergence of services into one."

Indeed, this push and pull has created a different efficiency and service model for some companies. These businesses are reassessing the role of the intermediary. Rather than cutting back to gain efficiencies on the product side, they are bundling the suite of offerings provided by their channel intermediaries in order to offer a "one-stop shop" of value. These companies derive similar efficiencies from the consolidation, but the focus has shifted to the customer. The rise

As one executive stated, those who are in the best position to control the customer hold the key to the future.

of "relationship managers" at banks and other financial services institutions serves as one example of this. As one executive stated, those who are in the best position to control the customer hold the key to the future.

Business leaders who wish to evolve to a more customer-centric organization will look to value creation in various parts of their enterprise.

Among their considerations will be:

❑ Optimizing the collection and use of information;
❑ Fully exploiting core investments;
❑ Improving customer share as well as market share;
❑ Maintaining excellent customer service as a core strength if not a core competency.

Something as seemingly simple as instituting a pay-as-you-go system for information technology (IT) processes, applications, and infrastructure instead of a single fixed-cost customer investment is one approach that a large computer software company is taking to offer its customers a new value model. It's an idea designed after the electrical utility concept and differs from existing outsourcing and hosting services in three ways:

❑ It is shared,
❑ It is standardized, and
❑ It is scalable.

The changes being pioneered offer stakeholders improved flexibility and control. Agile businesses often design additional value into their business models.

Optimizing the Collection and Use of Information

Since the advent of data-mining techniques, companies have made headway in their awareness and use of customer data.

> **Agile businesses take the time to read the tea leaves of their own customer data.**

Yet, studies indicate that businesses still under-collect, under-synthesize, and under-leverage the vast amounts of information they collect enterprise-wide on customers. Agile businesses take the time to read the tea leaves of their own customer data.

eBay has made this an art form. In fact, CEO Meg Whitman actively involves eBay's customers in the handling of customer support, product development, and business strategy. When eBay introduces new features or functionality, it carefully observes chat rooms and auction behavior to determine how successful the pickup has been. In addition, Whitman regularly convenes focus groups of active users of the site to solicit feedback, which eBay then directly channels back into the continuous refinement of the company. In effect, what eBay has done so successfully is incorporate its vast army of users into an active, real-time information loop. As such, eBay's users serve as informal "workers" as well as customers.

Promoting Organizational Recycling of Core Investments

True customer-focused organizations have embraced the wealth of information they can derive from their cross-channel activity and translate that into tangible improvements in terms of customer intimacy. These organizations place a premium on fully exhausting core investments. Last season's hit niche product can be this season's repurposed, remarketed, cross-channel titan.

Les Moonves, the new president and chief executive of CBS Television, offers one example of this kind of strategic thinking. He and his team recently closed a deal with their station affiliates that will allow the network to repurpose up to five hours of prime time content. He's taking a similar look at the CBS/Paramount library and, in a recent article, stated, "I don't think we have tapped into the library like we possibly could with all of these outlets." He adds, "There are a great bunch of properties available that we can possibly tap into and go back a little ways with."

Some other companies approach the inward search for value from the opposite direction, by adopting the concept of self-cannibalization. By way of definition, self-cannibalization occurs when a company deliberately introduces a product that directly competes with or challenges a traditional property. For instance, if Campbell's Soup decided to introduce freeze-dried packs of soup it would likely lose some of its core "canned soup" customers to the newer product. Despite the seeming illogic, self-cannibalization can be a strong strategy in commoditized markets where consumers' need for innovation drives companies to adapt portions of their core business. In so doing, agile companies will still seek to represent their core strengths. In the hypothetical Campbell's Soup example, the business dynamics did not change—it was still selling soup—but the packaging and the impression have.

Whatever the specifics of one's chosen approach, the notion should clearly be on strategies that extend brand over approaches that are innovative simply to be innovative. By more fully exploiting core assets, a company may succeed in intelligently strengthening and extending brand capability.

Improving Customer Share as Well as Market Share

The relationship with the customer is sometimes more important than the product or the service because the relationship is the gateway to future sales. Agile businesses have brought discernment to the quest for market share. They understand that penetrating top-tier, high-profitability customers often provides greater value than the traditional pursuit of market share for market share's sake.

As we have learned in the last decade, market share alone does not beget profitability. Profitable customers create profitability. The customer loyalty movement that began a few years ago captures this spirit. Yet, it is often the case in practice that employees are better rewarded for the successful hunt and capture of new deals than they are for the resourceful plumbing of current high-value customers. Add to the fact that the cost of acquiring a new customer is significantly higher than hanging onto an existing one, and there's even more reason to identify and prioritize valued relationships.

Vodafone is one of the world's largest wireless companies. CEO Chris Gent informed us that 20% of his customers accounted for 60% of his revenues. Recognizing this, Vodafone's emphasis is now on exploiting effective customer relationship management tools and systems to gain a larger share of the most valuable sector of the market. As Gent states, "Customers who aren't spending money don't do us much good because it costs us money to acquire them. We've considered this quite carefully and focused our efforts on customers who will spend money with us." The results seem to speak for themselves. "In a difficult trading year," says Gent, "we've improved margins by three percentage points."

Maintaining Excellent Customer Service

In a market contraction, customer service tends to serve as a ready target for the first round of employee cuts. Those who have attempted to make airline reservations directly with the major airlines in the economic aftermath of the September 11 disaster may have experienced the ramifications of those cutbacks firsthand as average hold times skyrocketed.

For most industries, while customer retention is important

in a market up-cycle, it is never more important than in a downturn. Customer satisfaction is a premium retention tool in a contraction and must be nurtured accordingly. That said, help desks and customer support services are simply not a core competency for many companies. Their business is generally product- or service-based. So too their competencies. For them, outsourcing some or all of the customer support service may be a sensible way to ensure consistent, high quality while containing the costs associated with its provision.

Customer satisfaction is a premium retention tool in a contraction and must be nurtured accordingly.

Agile businesses understand that they must constantly adapt in the pursuit of value. They understand that digital transformation has allowed them to increase the number of customer touch points and they make a practice of thoughtfully distilling the information these touch points provide on their customers' needs and wants. Most importantly, agile businesses understand that the customer value continuum is refreshed and sustained by those companies that assiduously seek to orient their business around the evolving needs of their key customers and constituents.

Agile businesses also recognize that they not only have a responsibility to provide value to their customers and constituents directly through more meaningful products and services, but they also have an obligation to unlock, manage, and report on the value of key intellectual assets so that investors and other key stakeholders may more clearly understand the full measure of a company's worth.

SEARCHING FOR VALUE IN THE INTANGIBLE

Our new economy has given rise to the intangible. Market valuations have soared, businesses conceived, patents delivered on the basis of something as airy and invisible as a concept. Not only has this been true in the U.S., but it has also been the case in many other countries throughout the world. In this knowledge economy, extraordinary advances in technology have placed an extraordinary premium on information. Personal shopping habits and demographic information now provide businesses with a degree of customer profiling never before possible, allowing them to tailor advertising, products, and services to an exquisite degree.

Implicit in this is the notion of value. We know intangible assets such as personal information, brand, and goodwill have value, but how much and how does one calculate what is inherently subjective? These questions have become part of the ongoing debate as the first blush of the new economy has subsided.

Intangibles cover a broad swath of assets, but the primary class falls into the category of intellectual property, a category that includes many items. Among them are:

- ❏ Patents
- ❏ Brands
- ❏ Publications
- ❏ Distribution systems
- ❏ Methodologies
- ❏ Research and development, and
- ❏ Customer lists.

195

The potential value of these investments can be surprising. Take brand value. A report by *Business Week* indicated that Apple Computer's brand value accounted for a whopping 80% of its market capitalization. Similarly, according to Alan M. Webber's article in *Fast Company*—"New Math for a New Economy"—the SABRE reservation system developed by American Airlines represented half of parent company, AMR's, market value in 2000. (The other half was tangible assets, such as 700 multimillion-dollar airliners and lucrative airport gate contracts.) Better yet, most of those intangible assets often don't depreciate. You don't wear out research or run out of brand power—at least most of the time.

Seeing the Value

What a company does with its innovation, how it manages and utilizes intellectual property assets in conjunction with all of its other assets, can shape commercial success. But oftentimes value is hidden. One study determined that 67% of U.S. companies own technology they fail to exploit. This is often because the asset may not be seen to have immediate use or the company may not have the resources needed to effectively deploy it.

Even companies that go to the trouble of patenting their advancements often fail to use them to their potential. The research company BTG estimated that 35% of patented technologies go to waste. The lost value of those wasted technologies? BTG put that at more than $115 billion. Others cite economic data indicating that for every $1 invested in R&D, shareholder valued increases by $10 and say the opportunity cost should be higher. If they are correct, that would put the total underutilized asset value at $1 trillion.

In contrast, agile businesses are aggressive in their pursuit of value, both organic and derived. With the emergence of intangibles as a more widely recognized value category, these adaptive organizations have seized them as a strategic means of capturing and unlocking monetary value from these already owned but possibly underutilized or undervalued investments.

Agile businesses we have observed generate value from their intellectual property in a number of ways:

❑ *Develop new products and services for resale*: A company may be able to extract additional dollars from its intellectual property by developing products or services that deepen their core competencies, so long as the resource and development effort do not harm the company's current competitive position or adversely affect its longer-term business goals.

❑ *License out*: If the intellectual property is determined to fall outside of the company's core activities but may be useful in the future, licensing or cross-licensing to a third party can be a lucrative way to recoup value without draining critical resources.

❑ *Create joint venture or strategic alliance*: If a technology is deemed viable in the future, but a company's goals or resources make short-term use impractical, then a joint venture or strategic alliance may be a good approach.

❑ *Sell*: In those cases where a particular intellectual property is non-core and the company sees no possible future use for it, the IP may be an ideal candidate for sale. What your company cannot use could be valuable to another.

❏ *Spin out*: Similarly, a spinout may be ideal for a non-core technology that would contribute substantial value as a stand-alone business.

❏ *Donate*: If the intellectual property is immature and the company is not interested in developing it further, it may consider donating it to a non-profit research institution or university. The company can then reap value from the tax benefit.

Assessing Value

The rise of intellectual property as a key asset has, in some ways, outpaced the market's ability to respond to the challenge of determining an appropriate value.

The rise of intellectual property as a key asset has, in some ways, outpaced the market's ability to respond to the challenge of determining an appropriate value.

As the center of gravity of our economies has shifted from manufacturing-based to knowledge-based, the assets most related to value and growth have also shifted from physical to intangible. This shift is not sudden. Rather, it's been growing for nearly a century. For example, in 1929, the proportion of intangible business capital compared with tangible business capital was 30% versus 70%. In 1990, the proportion was 63% to 37%. Moreover, this shift has outpaced traditional financial reporting practices.

For example, America Online has spent more than a billion dollars attracting its user base. And no one doubts that that outlay of funds was largely responsible for AOL's value and growth. Yet current financial reporting practices typically require companies to keep this type of value off their balance sheets until a company is either bought or sold. Some companies like 3M have sought ways to work around such limits in order to illuminate the value of their R&D more clearly to investors. 3M reports on what it calls "innovation revenues," in which it records the sales generated from products released in the previous four years.

Another area often overlooked is the investment companies make in joint ventures and alliances. The number of these types of partnerships flourished in the last half decade, fueled by the reasonable understanding that an agreed-upon network of key supply or value chain partners meant that companies could offer their customers complete, vetted solutions. In the hurry to tie down high-quality alliances, however, many companies paid scant attention to measuring the return on investment. How much do the joint ventures cost to support? What is the incremental revenue stream they provide? This type of information could be tremendously useful to all parties.

As we'll see later in the chapter, assessing value more closely is a trend that will increasingly become the norm. But, of course, to assess value well, companies must first know what they have in their closet.

Taking Inventory

In many organizations, the effective development and use of innovation and intangibles are the primary force driving corporate success and shareholder value. However, many organizations don't maintain a listing of their intangible assets—what assets they own, how they're being protected, how they're creating value for the company. Other companies might list their legally registered patents, trademarks, and copyrights, but lack accessible information on how these assets are being used. And most companies have few formal guidelines in place to govern the use and management of valuable trade secrets and related confidential information.

Given the importance agile businesses place on leveraging value, taking inventory is a prerequisite. It involves:

❑ Assessing current intellectual property,
❑ Assessing whether it is being used and how,
❑ Determining if the asset should be licensed or sold,
❑ Determining if and how the asset is being protected.

By more carefully monitoring the use and accountability for their intangible assets, agile businesses can help ensure they reap better advantage from their investment.

A recent survey of global companies across industries conducted by KPMG sought an executive perspective on how best to manage an intellectual property portfolio. Among the measures they considered best practices were:

❑ Maintaining a precise intellectual property asset inventory;

❏ Establishing the value of that portfolio;

❏ Developing a clear and integrated intellectual property management strategy; and

❏ Supporting the strategy with the right structure and processes to ensure all aspects of key intellectual property are protected and maintained.

MAKING VALUE MORE TRANSPARENT

In the 1800s British investors were loath to invest in United States companies until these companies had adopted accounting standards commensurate with Britain's well-developed principles. Investors were looking for a format that was predictable and proven in order to better evaluate a company's investment prospects. Standards were approved and have been a part of U.S. accounting practices ever since. The goal was transparency, providing investors with a window into a company to more clearly understand the quality of that company's performance. But, the double-edged sword with standards is that unless they are refreshed to keep pace with changes in the market, the very transparency they are intended to create for investors will be obscured.

Such transparency is the heart of current ongoing discussion in the financial community, among accounting firms, investors, analysts, and the SEC,

> But, the double-edged sword with standards is that unless they are refreshed to keep pace with changes in the market, the very transparency they are intended to create for investors will be obscured.

in light of recent corporate failings and restatements. The process of making financial reporting more germane to today's business environment had emerged as a matter of intense debate even before the demise of Enron, but the seriousness of that company's collapse has unequivocally catapulted the subject to center stage.

One clear output from that debate is the acknowledgment that the nation's current system of financial reporting is outdated. More complete disclosure of intangibles and trends and more current reporting of key performance metrics are needed to ensure less volatility, more accurate stock valuations, and better investor protection. As Harvey Pitt, the new chairman of the Securities and Exchange Commission, concluded in remarks to the American Institute of Certified Public Accountants, "quarterly and annual reports are static ... often stale" and "not always capable of being deciphered by sophisticated experts, much less ordinary investors."

Many accounting firms, including KPMG, agree. As Steve Butler, recent chairman of KPMG, stated in a press release on the subject, "It's finally time to move the accounting model of the Industrial Age into the Information Age. Specifically, we can no longer ignore the intangible assets of knowledge-based companies or be satisfied with a leisurely, quarterly, after-the-fact reporting cycle. Even a perfect audit of less-than-relevant and out-of-date information will not do investors much good."

It is clear, particularly in light of Enron and the concern

this has raised among many of the nation's chief executives, audit committees, boards of directors, and legions of investors, that financial reporting standards need to more transparently:

❑ Describe business operations,

❑ Account for intangible assets,

❑ Disclose leading indicators and trends (many of which are nonfinancial), and

❑ Better inform investors about risks and opportunities.

Many in the financial community, including KPMG, also believe there needs to be greater focus on how financial information is distributed to investors. Retrospective analyses of performance in today's quarterly reporting model must give way to real-time reporting. Once real-time reporting is in place, it will enable the audit emphasis to switch to error prevention rather than after-the-fact detection. Such a switch would make the auditing process more relevant and more meaningful.

The other structural change that needs to occur is also one acknowledged by the broader financial community. The Financial Accounting Standards Board (FASB), the designated private sector organization in the U.S. that establishes financial accounting and reporting standards, must act more swiftly to address flaws in current accounting practices that have the harmful effect of offering less disclosure than is needed. In concert with this, the investor community, notably absent today, needs to be brought more closely into the standards-setting process.

THE ADVANTAGES OF BETTER REPORTING ON INTANGIBLES

Intangibles rise to the fore in all discussions concerning the refinement of financial reporting practices because of their tremendous but often uncaptured value. As the previous section articulated, the primary reason for improvements in this area is the provision of greater insight to investors on the strength and performance of the companies they're invested in. Less well known but extremely important is the tangible value such increased disclosure provides to businesses themselves.

One of the preeminent voices on this subject is Baruch Lev, the Bardes Professor of Accounting at New York University's Stern School of Business. Professor Lev was kind enough to speak with us in the course of writing this book.

Recent studies conducted under Lev at NYU have shown that intangible-intensive companies are frequently undervalued. In one particular study, Lev and his colleagues examined the risk-adjusted future returns of a select group of intangible-heavy companies. By using the risk-adjusted rate, the researchers knew that if the intangibles were properly valued, mathematics would dictate that the (risk-adjusted) rate should be zero. In actuality, however, what they found was that the rate for most of the intangible-intensive companies was positive, by two or three points. The positive finding indicated that the full value of the company was not being reflected and that the company was, in effect, undervalued.

The cause of the undervaluation, according to Lev and others in the financial community who have been active in examining the issue, has to do with information asymmetry and the relationship between risk and uncertainty. Information asymmetry? The term may sound pretty esoteric, but its evidence is all around us.

Take the process of buying a car. Nowadays, most prospective car buyers can readily track down the invoice price for the automobile they're considering purchasing. But before this advance consumers went into the transaction fairly blind. Since they did not know what the car cost the dealer, they could not be entirely sure of the car's worth. All they had to go on was the dealer's pitch, the price that other dealers were prepared to sell the car for, and information from their friends who may have bought the same make or model. From a negotiating standpoint, this left most consumers to "guesstimate" the value. Dealers had all of the necessary information at their disposal. They knew the cost of the car and the margins they hoped to make. Their primary variable was simply determining how much the customer was willing to pay.

That is how information asymmetry displays itself. It occurs when certain relevant information is known to some parties involved in a transaction, but not all. In financial markets, the issue has become a value problem with the increasing but largely unreported weight of intangible assets on corporate balance sheets. "Information asymmetry has a very

> "Information asymmetry has a very negative effect on markets, on trade, and on social institutions," says Lev.

negative effect on markets, on trade, and on social institutions," says Lev. "Three Nobel laureates in economics got their awards based on proving this point."

The reason it presents a value problem for investors is easy to divine. Shareholders don't know if what they're paying for a stock is too high or too low. How good a deal, or not, did they get? Less obvious, but keenly important, is the impact of this value and information disconnect on companies themselves. Studies have shown that a company's cost of capital increases or decreases depending on how open and transparent they are in discussing their business. Less doubt means less risk. Less risk means cheaper capital.

The lesson, therefore, is that in dollars and cents terms, both companies and investors stand to gain through a more complete assessment and reporting of value. For intangible-intensive companies, the benefits of doing so can result in:

❑ Lower cost of capital,
❑ A higher rate of investment, which would support future innovation,
❑ More efficient resource allocation, and
❑ A better sense of true return on investment.

Although many hold the view that intangibles and intellectual property issues pertain primarily to the high-technology industry, other industries—such as pharmaceuticals, defense, financial services, and even manufacturing—also have a large portion of their assets tied to intangibles and stand to reap the rewards of improved disclosure.

Lev recounted one example of this with us when he described some work he had done with a large pharmaceutical company. The company was being "hammered" by financial analysts and given very unfavorable reviews. At some point, Lev recalls, "the company finally became fed up." The company called a huge conference with financial analysts in which they provided "detailed information about their product pipeline, expected launch dates, even expected revenues." The response was telling. When Lev looked at the reports analysts filed after the conference, the comments were "incredibly positive, extremely favorable."

CONCLUSION

Agile businesses are constantly adapting in the pursuit of value. The companies that best achieve this continuously orient their business around the evolving needs of their key customers and constituents. In this way, the customer value continuum is refreshed and sustained. Mindful of resource efficiency and leverage, these businesses also seek to exploit the untapped potential of their intellectual property portfolio. In this way, the value of their innovation and distinctive knowledge is captured and utilized. Finally, as the financial reporting community works to update accounting standards trailing rapid market advances, agile businesses understand that they can best serve their investors and their own business interests by carefully assessing, monitoring, and disclosing the impact of their brands, their innovation, and their future prospects. In this way the value of their business is better appraised and understood.

···

CHAPTER ELEVEN

Agile Redux

W e have talked at length about agility in its different business guises and contexts. This chapter seeks to distill some of the key approaches that distinguish agile businesses and constitute a more competitively sustainable operating environment.

INDUSTRY INSIGHTS, EXPERIENCE FROM THE TRENCHES

Since Internet mania propelled much of the last decade's economic growth, it makes sense that the high-technology community should have found itself first to ride the 30-foot swells created by the boom and first to come hurtling down at the other side. This unique, if heart-in-throat perspective, offers insight on ways to navigate future market volatility. And while some of the wisdom may have been borne on the back of high technology, it is knowledge nonetheless widely applicable to other industries traveling the same course. Collectively, we gain a glimmer of the future shape of sustainable agility.

There is first the recognition that our business hegemony has been changed. Jeff Shuman, a professor of management and director of entrepreneurial studies at Bentley College, remarked, "The balance of power in business relationships has shifted to the customers, be they manufacturers or end-users." Tom Siebel agrees. "It used to be," he says, "that you could do business with a bank any way you wanted to, as long as it was in one of its branches. You could buy a car from Ford any way you wanted to, as long as it was through one of its distributors.... That is the way the world used to work. We used to tell the customer how to do business with us. Now we will do business with our customers any way they want."

> **The convergence vision of the last decade has come under pressure to achieve a single point of nexus around the consumer.**

This is because technological advancements have empowered the customer to an unprecedented degree. Customers expect more and demand more. The convergence vision of the last decade has come under pressure to achieve a single point of nexus around the consumer. This reality in turn is having implications on forms of corporate collaboration and corporate business models.

Business Models

Although it may be clear that the customer is the heart of the modern enterprise, what is murkier is the degree of customization in place. The media industry has pointed a spotlight on the need for business model improvements, a need other market segments are also feeling. Media and entertainment companies have been at the forefront of this realization due to the severity of the advertising shutdown and the fact that their businesses are often particularly sensitive to customer buying swings. To first satisfy and then retain customers, media and other companies will be modifying their current business models to deliver, on the one hand, more appropriate pricing and tailored products and, on the other, more effective customer retention, customer win-back, and customer share techniques.

Variable pricing will give way to value pricing as customers more closely scrutinize return on investment. In lieu of or as an adjunct to advertising revenues, some businesses may seek to explore subscription or flat fees for their services. Terri Santisi, the global director of KPMG's Media and Entertainment practice, adds, "The responsibility of media (and other) companies will be to make tools that empower the consumers." As a consequence, services that provide real-time, anywhere, anytime access will earn a higher premium than the more traditional, point-in-time, device-bound alternatives.

That said, many companies are still short of being able to offer their customers the real-time, accurate information and customization they seek. For businesses still in the throes of their own digital transformation, the ongoing test will be for them to assess the customer value impact of each of their core processes. As Shuman states, "The challenge facing all businesspeople is to disregard how their business works today, to discard their legacy thinking, and then work backward through the value creation process, developing an understanding of when, where, and how value is created." Agile businesses will increasingly make that their mission.

What it adds up to, according to many, is simplicity. "We have all become victims of admiring the Internet," says Terry Carrick, Director of Marketing for the New York company, Mediapages. He believes that this has caused us to wander away from the straightforward, sound management practice of knowing what our customer-centric focus is. "For example," Carrick notes, "people still want to kick tires, but (in the online world) we haven't taken care of the trust factor you get in a face-to-face transaction."

For some of the answers, we're looking to the software community.

Coalescence and Collaboration

From its earliest roots as Arpanet, the Internet has served as a means of knowledge sharing, first among scientists, academics, and members of the defense community and later, of course, by commercial enterprises throughout the world.

Over time, the software community advanced these connective technologies in ways designed to make information more meaningful, through enterprise resource planning and supply chain management, and in ways designed to make market activity more efficient, through the explosion in business marketplaces.

The mature fusing of these efforts has more recently resulted in a concept known as *collaborative commerce*. Still relatively new to many companies, collaborative commerce combines business intelligence systems with the value chain fluidity of the exchange. The results are better integration, better leverage, better transparency, and better customer interaction.

Take Seagate Technology. Seagate, the world's largest manufacturer of disk drives and magnetic heads, partnered with integration software specialist, TIBCO, one of Reuters' companies, to build a global order fulfillment system. By deploying enterprise hubs and e-marketplaces to connect suppliers, distributors, and partners, Seagate is able to connect both customers and partners into its internal business systems seamlessly and internationally. The benefits are twofold: lower fulfillment costs and improved customer satisfaction.

Many companies that have made significant investments in diverse technologies over the past several years are now looking to take more complete advantage of their investment. "The marketplace," says Avaya's McGuire, "is looking at solutions not discrete products." This is true of both corporate buyers as well as their end-users. Whereas bells and whistles may have driven some of the technology purchasing decisions in the past, value-conscious companies are now placing the real premium on integration benefits.

Business Week cites the story of Procter & Gamble. The *Fortune* 31 giant produces and markets three hundred of the world's top consumer product brands across an increasingly diffuse global network. That kind of volume can make efficient product development a challenging endeavor. To reduce duplication of effort and instill better control, P&G engaged software maker MatrixOne to automate the company's product development function. Now, among other things, developers can sift through a massive database containing 200,000 different product designs. The resource allows employees throughout P&G's global enterprise to leverage prior work. The results have cut the company's development times by 50%.

In contrast to some of the unrealized promises of the last decade's technological wizardry, the results of collaborative commerce have proven measurable and tangible. The Yankee Group estimates that collaborative commerce will save U.S. companies $223 billion by 2006 through improved inventories and production cost savings. We predict that collaborative commerce will emerge as a sustaining strategy for agile businesses for its role in enabling both operational efficiency and market growth.

The Yankee Group estimates that collaborative commerce will save U.S. companies $223 billion by 2006.

Profitability Enhancement Through Margin Enhancement

Operational efficiency and market share growth must be tied to profitability, something that concerns all companies, particularly in volatile times. Certainly the communications industry has witnessed its share of tumult over the past several years. Whether from deregulation and privatization, increased competitive pressure, or the broadband buildup, the upheaval has made the industry especially keen on profitability.

Catalyzed by the particular complexity of billing and revenue collecting arrangements, communications companies are becoming ever more skilled in margin enhancement. It is a drive that will increasingly thread across industries and become a mainstay strategy.

Margins used to be a secondary priority for most communications companies, protected by locked-in rates and minimal competition. When this changed and markets opened to renewed competition, these companies were required to look beyond a narrow revenue view to one that encompassed profitable growth. They discovered that processes for managing costs and growing the top line were not coordinated. They also observed that multi-party vendors and other external touch points were creating the opportunity for revenue and cost leakage.

The communications industry was, of course, far from alone in this matter. But as Carl Geppert, Partner and Director of KPMG's Americas Communications practice, notes, "With communications companies facing a treacherous operating environment, there was a need to adopt a holistic and aggressive approach to enhancing margins." Accordingly, the communications industry has, in many ways, set the pace for new best practices in margin enhancement.

Leading practitioners suggest that margin enhancement can be achieved most successfully by performing a careful end-to-end assessment on processes that contribute to revenue, cost, and profitability. For example, a revenue assessment might track how effectively and comprehensively a company reconciles its service orders from ordering through provisioning to billing and collection. A cost assessment might encompass a review that ranges from vendor contracts through service ordering to invoice reconciliation and financial processing. And a profitability enhancement review might seek to examine the effectiveness (or existence) of activities that assess revenue, costs, and margins by product, service, customer, and geography.

One leading U.S. competitive local exchange carrier employed these techniques to get a better handle on how to improve gross margins on key customers. Using better-defined margin enhancement practices, the company reviewed the data and assumptions that went into gross margin calculations. It looked at the impact of customer credits and adjustments and the impact of current customer service agreement commitments. The resulting discipline enabled the company to better assess and manage its customer activation and billing policies and processes.

Current margin enhancement practices focus on identifying possible revenue and cost leaks. Here are some of the red flags experts suggest watching for:

❏ Government deregulation or privatization. This inevitably alters the competitive landscape and heightens pricing and quality pressures.
❏ Significant organizational, process, personnel, or systems changes. This can result in weakened controls.
❏ Poor integration or reconciliation of core revenue and cost application systems.

❏ Significant merger activity. This can result in redundant business processes, systems, and headcount as well as revenue process change management issues.

❏ Significant reliance on vendors or competitors to achieve critical revenue and cost process objectives. This places the balance of risk outside management's direct control.

❏ Increasing bad debts and aging of receivables.

❏ Shrinking profit margins combined with inadequate information on the actual cost of one's products or services.

Margin enhancement issues often involve more than a review of internal business processes and systems. They also involve third parties other than the traditional end-user customer. In ironing out any kinks raised by these networks, save yourself time and look for root causes, not symptoms. Repeated corrections indicate that the underlying problem has not been addressed.

Although fairly new as a formal pursuit, margin enhancement best practices will become increasingly important to other industries beyond communications. Complex sectors with dispersed value chains, high-transaction volumes, and heavy reliance on information technology such as the health care, pharmaceutical, and financial services industries make obvious candidates.

These segments will be attracted to the fact that margin enhancement efforts are quantifiable in terms of revenue generated, revenue recovered, cost savings, and improved margins. Better yet, as data from communications companies shows, the revenue and savings captured from such efforts often represent a multiple of the costs incurred in carrying out the analyses. Formal integrated margin enhancement practices will emerge as an important sustaining strategy for agility.

Steady, Calm Acceleration

After media, software, and communications, the electronics industry represents the fourth major component of the high technology industry. Just as each of the prior three has taught us something about the future shape of business agility, the seasoned cyclicals, such as semiconductor chip manufacturers, teach us about longevity. These weathered companies know not to cut the lifeboats at the first sign of economic distress. Too often, short-term cost management and revenue generation decisions have lasting negative long-term effects. Instead, veterans of previous economic down-cycles show us how to manage lean and plan for growth even when growth prospects seem remote.

> **The executives that we spoke with all agree that you tackle the areas with the highest impact and highest potential for profitability first.**

One of the key learnings is risk-based prioritization. The executives that we spoke with all agree that you tackle the areas with the highest impact and highest potential for profitability first, while incubating longer-term opportunities. This is particularly true during a market downturn.

Since it is often not immediately apparent what products, services, or initiatives might rise to the top, this is not necessarily as simple as it might sound. Amongst other considerations, the decision on what to tackle first should hinge on an assessment of the significance and likelihood of key business risks that could impair the initiative's success.

Such risks could include the viability of a crucial component supplier during the downturn or the viability of the market sector targeted by a given initiative (dot.coms provide an all too convenient example). Other factors could include aggressive competitor pricing, the relative complexity of the product or service, and the corresponding impact on the length of the sales cycle, error rate, and training times. All companies deal with these issues as part of their management responsibilities. Seasoned cyclicals, however, have simply had more times at bat dealing with issues exacerbated by a market contraction.

As a consequence, the most successful cyclicals understand that a consistent, measured approach to growth is the desired objective. Hypergrowth is euphoric—and who would not be tempted to open one's door wide to it?—but hypergrowth is also very hard to manage. Investors become quickly attached to a 34% growth rate, but from an efficiency standpoint one is usually racing too hard to be fastidiously mindful of exactly where the dollars are coming from or going to.

A sporadic, wobbly growth curve also brings headaches. Aside from the obvious uncertainty, it can be difficult to build business for the long term when capital, share prices, and costs move so unpredictably.

Consistency breeds confidence. From experience, cyclicals understand that to persuade investors to ride out the downside of a market curve means that those investors must sustain a reasonable degree of confidence that the company's prospects are sound. The virtue of a steady hand on the accelerator is that it breeds familiarity and trust. Expectations are managed.

John Maynard Keynes might have said, "In the long term, we're all dead," but believing in the future requires an act of faith. Agile businesses believe in the long term by placing faith in themselves and by proving their credibility through consistent, considered growth.

Passion

Finally, the high-tech community as a whole offers a lesson in the very passion it has brought to the wave of technological advances that swept so much of the global economy over the past several years. Young careerists have often traditionally been advised to keep emotion out of business. Be cool. Be objective. The reality, however, is that some of today's most successful executives are strident in their conviction that passion is central to success in our undulating global marketplace. Passion kindles energy, effort, resourcefulness, and creativity and ignites the will to succeed—all characteristics that helped charm and sweep the masses into seeing the possibilities of digital transformation and its potential for the future.

Passion is tied to momentum. "When people are passionate about being number one," says Vodafone's Chris Gent, "that really helps us." That kind of conviction fosters positive morale, strong internal unity, and a collective sense of purpose.

Companies compete on strong fundamentals, but it is often the degree of fervency that separates the good from the great. Some runners lean forward to break the ribbon. Others don't. In the difference, races are won or lost.

Murray Thom is familiar with the ups and downs of business. A former managing director of CBS Records in New Zealand turned entrepreneur, Thom credits passion with allowing him to persevere in the face of adversity. "When you are passionate about something," he says, "you tend to feel tenacious—it's something you want to do." Where some businesses might throw in the towel after a major defeat, leaders with passion and conviction are, as Thom says, "masters at encouraging themselves." When Team Canada's hockey squad talked about what it would take to win at the 2002 Winter Olympics, they said they would rely upon "controlled emotion" and a "deep, down adrenaline rush that they could call on when needed." They went home with gold.

Companies compete on strong fundamentals, but it is often the degree of fervency that separates the good from the great.

So many of Silicon Valley's legendary garage enterprises were sustained based on the sheer emotional will of their founders and employees. Their staggering hours and work intensity were driven from within, from an active intellectual interest and a fundamental belief in the value of ideas. While the rest of the world may have been carried away by the exuberance, there's no denying that the "I can do and be anything" culture generated tremendously high productivity.

Although today's businesses operate in a more disciplined, sober environment, competitively nimble organizations recognize that a company with the right policies, the best communication flow, and the most refined practices still needs to channel the enthusiasm and motivation of its workforce to claim the performance edge. Gent adds, "People want to be star performers. In our business, their massive competitive instincts are a critically important driver."

The marketplace rewards passion, energy, initiative, and independent thought. Those companies that use these emotions and skills to hold together an already strong business will find it much easier to harness agility and traverse the competitive terrain.

CONCLUSION

Keeping pace with an ever-changing environment is critical to the evolutionary success of all organisms. Survival depends on rapid adaptation. For businesses, that means an ability to cultivate change in ways that are intelligently aligned with one's business skills and goals. Such is the nature of competition. Agile businesses will seek to curb the blows of a roiling marketplace by strengthening their fundamentals, streamlining their core, and tenaciously identifying opportunities to create growth.

They do this by moving deliberately but thoughtfully.

Agile businesses will seek to curb the blows of a roiling marketplace by strengthening their fundamentals, streamlining their core, and tenaciously identifying opportunities to create growth.

There is the adage that the sharp knife tears less. In their desire for consistent, measured growth, agile businesses do not confine cost reductions to weaker economic times. Rather they make it a constant discipline. So too for growth. Reflexive "me too" competitive responses to product planning or marketing are avoided when growth strategies are implemented and refined continually. When these strategies are tied to value and profitability measures, as opposed to those strategies that are strictly top-line or market share related, a company can make process enhancement a continual practice.

To make this happen, agile businesses understand they need people. Internally, we know that consistent growth in today's demanding marketplace requires unusually strong managerial talent. Not every company has it. Leading executives monitor their team's readiness and recalibrate accordingly. Top managers rely on their employee base, not only to execute on initiatives, but to serve as active owners of their projects. They provide their line managers with a vested, considered interest in the cost and growth performance of their programs, knowing that empowerment motivates and integration makes a team. In this way, agile businesses rely on an energetic, enthusiastic, connected workforce to achieve their goals.

The strongest businesses also rely on their broad network of external constituents. They recognize clearly that, particularly when times are tough, people turn to those they trust. Leaders who regularly and honestly update analysts and shareholders on who they are, where they're headed, and why it makes sense, earn credibility. Leaders who invest in their brand, even when a market contraction might make such expenditures seem contrary to conventional wisdom, buy themselves a voice to make their vision heard.

Fundamental to the external network is the customer. As the dust kicked up by the New Economy's feverish rise has settled, the customer has emerged as the unquestioned royalty. Thoughtful businesses will work to continue to orient their processes and products in ways that provide their customers with meaningful, real-time, accurate information.

Agile businesses understand that their mission is to bring real value to their investors. They understand that this is achieved by making business practices and financial reporting transparent and clear. Ours is a knowledge economy. Ideas, seemingly ethereal, have tangible worth. Intellectual property and other information assets add significant value to an organization. Agile businesses seek to capture this value and report on it. In this way they benefit through lower capital costs and investors benefit through increased confidence.

The key to agility is to be proactive instead of reactive, continual instead of intermittent, holistic instead of ad hoc, transparent instead of opaque, and confident instead of hesitant. That's not hard, is it?

Bibliography

Atkins, Robert G., and Adrian J. Slywotzky. *Bring on the Recession.* Mercer Management Consulting, 2001.

Baumohl, Bernard. "How We Missed Signs of a Slowdown." *Time,* April 30, 2001. Beal, Dave. "Sizing up CEO Superstar Status. Is It Deserved?" *St Paul Pioneer Press,* June 24, 2001.

Bernstein, Peter L. *Against the Gods: The Remarkable Story of Risk.* Wiley & Sons, 1996.

Bianco, Anthony, and Louis Lavelle. "The CEO Trap." *Business Week,* Dec. 11, 2000.

Blair, Margaret M., and Steven M.H. Wallman. *Unseen Wealth—Report of the Brookings Task Force on Intangibles.* Brookings Institution Press, 2001.

Blaxill, Mark F., and Thomas M. Hout. "Make Decisions Like a Fighter Pilot." 1987. Reprinted in *Perspectives on Strategy from the Boston Consulting Group,* edited by Carl W. Stern and George Stalk, Jr. John Wiley & Sons, Inc., 1998, pp. 164-166. www.bcg.com.

Borge, Dan. *The Book of Risk.* Wiley & Sons, 2001.

Buckley, Peter J., and Pervez N. Ghauri. *The Internationalization of the Firm: A Reader,* second edition. International Thomson Business Press, 1999.

Byrnes, Nanette, and David Henry.. "Confused About Earnings?" *Business Week,* Nov. 26, 2001.

Chandrasekhar, R., R.C. Bagrodia,, and K. Ganesh. "Managing in a Mature Market." *Business Today,* Nov. 7, 1998.

Chang, Richard. "Turning Passion into Organizational Performance: The Role of Passion in Business Management and Leadership." *Training & Development,* May 2001.

Clayton, Matthew J., Hartzell, Jay C., and Joshua Rosenberg. "The Impact of CEO Turnover on Equity Volatility." Paper published August 2000. Finance Department Working Paper Series, Stern School of Business, New York University.

Cook, Colin, and Don Spitzer. *World Class Transactions: Insights into Creating Shareholder Value Through Mergers and Acquisitions.* KPMG Transaction Services, white paper. KPMG LLP, 2001.

Courtney, Hugh G. "Games Managers Should Play." *World Economic Affairs,* 2:1, Fall 1997

Courtney, Hugh, Jane Kirkland, and Patrick Viguerie. "Strategy Under Uncertainty."*Harvard Business Review,* November-December 1997.

Couzin, Jennifer. "Tick Tick Tick." *The Industry Standard,* April 16, 2001.

Coyne, Kevin P., and Somu Subramaniam. "Bringing Discipline to Strategy." *The McKinsey Quarterly,* 1996, Number 4.

Crouhy, Michel, Dan Galai, and Robert Mark. *Risk Management.* McGraw-Hill, 2001.

Downs, Alan. "The Truth About Layoffs." *Management Review.* American Management Associatio, October 1995.

Dreman, David. *Contrarian Investment Strategies: The Next Generation.* Simon & Schuster, 1998.

Dzilna, Dzintars. "Staffing Down the Central Services Idea." *Folio: The Magazine for Magazine Management.* Sept. 30, 1999.

Ehlers, John F. *Rocket Science for Traders: Digital Signal Processing Applications,* Wiley & Sons, 2001.

Eisenhardt, Kathy. "Redefining Business Challenges." World Economic Forum, 2002.

Elash, Daniel D., and James R. Long. "Lessons in Authentic Leadership." *The CEO Refresher,* www.refresher.com/ !authenticleadership.html.Essex, David. "Recruiting Through the Downturn," *IT World,* May 7, 2001.

Fabrikant, Geraldine. "Big Returns, Minus the Pleasantries," *New York Times,* Feb. 17, 2002.

Freeland, John, and Christopher Sprague. "Making Procurement Pay." *Business and Management Practices.* Best's Review Property/Casualty Edition, April 1999.

Friedman, Jeffrey A. "How Tax Departments Can Help in an Economic Downturn." KPMG LLP.

Gallagher, Jim. "Edward Jones Gets Survey's Top Spot." *St. Louis Post-Dispatch,* Jan. 22, 2002.

Garr, Doug. *IBM Redux: Lou Gerstner and the Business Turnaround of the Decade.* Harper Business, 1999.

Garten, Jeffrey E. *The Mind of the CEO.* Perseus Publishing, 2001.

Geppert, Carl. *Margin Enhancement: How Focusing on Revenue and Related Costs Can Help Produce Profits* KPMG LLP, 2001.

Gettler, Leon. "Why Boards Unerringly Select the Wrong Chief Executives." *The Age (Melbourne)*, Nov. 16, 2001.

Gilpin, Robert. *Global Political Economy: Understanding the International Economic Order.* Princeton University Press, 2001.

Greer, Charles R., Timothy C. Ireland, and John R. Wingender. "Contrarian Human Resource Investments and Financial Performance After Economic Downturns." *Journal of Business Research*, 52:3, 2001, pp. 249-261.

Gross, Neil. "Commentary: 'Valuing Intangibles' Is a Tough Job, but It Has to Be Done." *BusinessWeek*, Aug. 6, 2001.

Hannen, Michelle, and Emily Ross. "People: Leaders for All Seasons." *Business Review Weekly* (Australia), Jan. 10, 2002, 24:1, pp. 51-55.

Hawn, Carleen. "The Man Who Sees Around Corners." *Forbes*, Jan. 21, 2002.

Jones, Dick, "Hire During Slump, Profit Two Years Later," *Dick Jones Communications*, June 28, 2001.

Hogan, Suzanne. "Employees and Image: Bringing Brand Image to Life." Second Annual Strategic Public Relations Conference, Chicago, IL, 1997.

HomeCare Staff. "When Will the Internet Hit Home(Care)?" *HomeCare*. October 2000.

Ivy Sea Online. "Authenticity and Leadership: What's the Connection?" Ivy Sea, Inc. San Francisco, CA, www.ivy-sea.com.

Jones, Del. "Use Recession to Plan for Next Level." *USA Today*, Feb. 1, 2002.

Jones, Mark, "CEOs Struggle to Keep the Brand Alive," *InfoWorld*, Dec. 17, 2001.

Judge, Paul C. "How Will Your Company Adapt?" *Fast Company*, December 2001.

Khermouch, Gerry, Stanley Holmes, and Moon Ihlwan. "The Best Global Brands." Special Report. *Business Week*, Aug. 6, 2001.

Kindleberger, Charles P. *Manias, Panics, and Crashes: A History of Financial Crises*, 4th edition. John Wiley & Sons, 2000.

King, Julia. "Jobs for Life." *Computerworld*. Jan. 14, 2002.

Ko, Erick. "A Matter of Survival." *Asian Business*, March 1998.

Koller, Glenn. *Risk Assessment and Decision Making in Business and Industry: A Practical Guide.* CRC Press, 1999.

Kosterlitz, Julie. "What Went Wrong?" *The National Journal*, Jan. 4, 2002.

KPMG, Assurance and Advisory Services Center. *Achieving Measurable Improvement in a Changing World.* KPMG LLP, 2001.

KPMG, Assurance Practice. "Boosting the Bottom Line Through Cost Management." KPMG LLP, 2001.

KPMG Consulting. *Shared Services.* KPMG LLP, 2001.

KPMG, Information Risk Management Services and Assurance and Advisory Services Center. *New Strategies for Success in E-Business: Managing Risks to Protect Brand, Retain Customers, and Enhance Market Capitalization.* KPMG LLP, 2001.

"KPMG's Butler Outlines Constructive Reforms at Gathering of Energy Industry Executives." Press Release. KPMG LLP, Feb. 14, 2002.

Krugman, Paul. *The Return of Depression Economics*. W.W. Norton & Co., 2000.

Krugman, Paul. "The W Scenario." *New York Times*, Feb. 22, 2002.

Lev, Baruch. *Intangibles: Management, Measurement, and Reporting*. Brookings Institution Press, 2001.

MacGregor, Roy. "A Nation Fueled by Rage: Controlled Emotion." *National Post*. Feb. 20, 2002.

Mamis, Robert, A. "Trade Secrets." *Inc*. August 1982.

Manning, Margie. "Cash Is King: Amdocs, Commerce Stockpiling for Tough Economic Times." *St. Louis Business Journal*, Nov. 30, 2001.

Maruca, Regina Fazio. "How to Manage Team Egos." *Fast Company*, October 2000.

McCarthy, Mary Pat, Stuart Campbell, and Rob Brownstein. *Security Transformation: Digital Defense Strategies*, McGraw-Hill, 2001.

McDargh, Eileen. "Uncovering Soul in the Healthcare Setting." www.eileenmcdargh.com.

McNamee, Mike. "New Yardsticks for Investors." *Business Week*, Nov. 5, 2001.

Meeropol, Michael A. "A Tale of Two Tax Cuts." EPI Issue Brief #157. Economic Policy Intitute, May 7, 2001.

Melamed, Leo, with Bob Tamarkin. *Leo Malamed: Escape to the Futures*. Wiley & Sons, 1996.

Mendels, Pam. "From CIO to Corner Office," *Business Week*, special report, Sept. 6, 2001.

Metcalfe, Steve. "Water Takes on a New Liquidity." *Euromoney*, May 2001, 139-142.

Micklethwait, John, and Adrian Wooldridge. *A Future Perfect: The Challenge and Hidden Promise of Globalization.* Random House (Crown Business), 2000.

Miller, Thomas R., and Beverly J. Vaughan. "Messages from the Management Past: Classic Writers and Contemporary Problems." *SAM Advanced Management Journal,* Society for Advancement of Management, Winter 2001.

Mullins, Robert, and Neil Orman. "Firms Polish Image During 'Down' Time." *Silicon Valley/San Jose Business Journal,* May 28, 2001.

Peters, Edgar E. *Complexity, Risk, and Financial Markets.* John Wiley & Sons, 1999.

Phillips, Charles. "Investing for the Long Haul." *Optimize,* November 2001.

Posner, Bruce G. "Squeeze Play." *Inc.,* July 1990.

Prentice, Brad. "Cutting Costs Doesn't Mean Clipping Wings." *The Business Times* (Singapore), Feb. 5, 1999.

Reingold, Jennifer. "Who's Afraid of a Recession?" (Interview with Adrian Slywotzky.) *Fast Company,* March 2001.

Richards, Chester W. "Riding the Tiger: What You Really Do with OODA Loops." Version 3, July 11, 1998. www.belisarius.com/modern_business_strategy/richards/riding_the_tiger/tiger.htm.

Rieches, Ryan. "Using a Recession to Grow Your Business: What Smart Companies Know About Marketing in a Downturn." www.b2bmarketer.org/marketing_in_a_downturn.html.

Ries, Al, and Jack Trout. *Positioning: The Battle for Your Mind.* McGraw-Hill, 2000.

Rigby, Darrell. "Moving Upward in a Downturn." *Harvard Business Review*, June 2001.

Robbins, Stever. "What Is a CEO's Job Anyway?" *Expert.Zine*, June 2001.

Romero, Simon. "Tech Crash Yielding Glut of Bandwidth." *Toronto Star*, June 25, 2001.

Saporito, Bill. "K Mart's Blue Period." *Time*, Jan. 14, 2002.

Savill, Brett, and John Studley. "Is Content King? A Value Conundrum." *Telecommunications: International Edition*. June 1999.

Sheridan, John H. "Aligning Structure with Strategy." *Industry Week*. May 15, 1989.

Slater, Robert. *The New GE: How Jack Welch Revived an American Institution*. McGraw-Hill (Business One Irwin), 1993.

Smart, Tim. "Time for a Corporate Makeover?" *U.S. News & World Report*, Jan. 14, 2002.

Springsteel, Ian. "Tax E-ffiency." *CFO*, May 2001.

Staff. "Bell & Howell Information and Learning." *New Zealand Management*, December 2000.

Staff. "It's Only a Game," *The Economist*, June 15, 1996.

Staff. "Let The Bad Times Roll," *The Economist*, April 7, 2001.

Staff. "Managing the Downturn." *The Economist*, April 7, 2001.

Staff. "Snip, Snip, Oops!" *The Economist*, Oct. 13, 2001.

Staff. "There's No Advantage in Change for Change's Sake." *Marketing Week*, March 14, 2002.

Staff. "What's Left." *The Economist*, May 12, 2001.

Stalk, George, Jr., and Thomas M. Hout. *Competing Against Time: How Time-Based Competition Is Reshaping Global Markets.* Free Press, 1990.

Stevenson, Richard W. "End of Recession Is Seen, but Strength of Recovery Is Unclear." *New York Times*, Feb. 22, 2002.

Stewart, Thomas A. "One CEO's View from the Top." *Business 2.0*, Nov. 7, 2001.

Stringer, Judy. "Tech Firms Turning to Proven Managers When Hiring CEOs." *Crain's Cleveland Business.* April 16, 2001.

Surowiecki, James. "A Good CEO Is Not Hard to Find." *The New Yorker*, July 2, 2001.

Teichgraeber, Tara. "Completing the Puzzle." *The Business Journal* (Phoenix), Jan. 18, 2002.

Turner, Freda. "Six Ways Top Organizations Avoid Leadership Crisis." *The CEO Refresher*, 2001.

Webber, Alan M. "New Math for a New Economy." *Fast Company*, January/February 2000.

Williams, Sid E. "Lyceum: Persistency; A Lesson Learned from the Lowly Ant." *Today's Chiropractic*, 27:4, July/August 1998 pp.6-11.

Wilson, Thomas B. *Innovative Reward Systems for the Changing Workplace.* McGraw-Hill, 1994.

Yoffie, David B., and Michael A. Cusumano. "Building a Company on Internet Time: Lessons from Netscape." *California Management Review,* Spring 1999, 41:3.

Yoffie, David B., and Mary Kwak. "Lessons from the Dotcom Days." *Financial Times*, Oct. 1, 2001.

Index